ISRAEL AND JUDAH

SKETCH OF THE HISTORY

OF

ISRAEL AND JUDAH

BY

J. WELLHAUSEN
PROFESSOR AT MARBURG

THIRD EDITION

Wipf and Stock Publishers
150 West Broadway • Eugene OR 97401
2001

Sketch of the History of Israel & Judah, 3rd Edition

By Wellhausen, J.

ISBN: 1-57910-532-7

Reprinted by *Wipf and Stock Publishers*
150 West Broadway • Eugene OR 97401

Previously published by Adam & Charles Black, 1891.

PREFACE.

THE following Sketch first appeared as the article ISRAEL in the *Encyclopædia Britannica* in 1881. It was afterwards reprinted in 1885, as an appendix to the English translation of my *Prolegomena*. That volume is now out of print, and there were difficulties in the way of an immediate reissue of the *Prolegomena* which do not apply to a simple reprint of the historical sketch. Nor is there any intrinsic reason why the two should not be separated; the latter therefore now appears, for the third time, as an independent booklet.

Marburg in Hessen
4 Juli 1891

Ehrerbietig
Ihr
Wellhausen

CONTENTS.

CHAP.		PAGE
I.	THE BEGINNINGS OF THE NATION	1
II.	THE SETTLEMENT IN PALESTINE	24
III.	THE FOUNDATION OF THE KINGDOM, AND THE FIRST THREE KINGS	39
IV.	FROM JEROBOAM I. TO JEROBOAM II.	57
V.	THE LIFE OF MEN IN OLD ISRAEL	70
VI.	THE FALL OF SAMARIA	81
VII.	THE DELIVERANCE OF JUDAH	94
VIII.	THE PROPHETIC REFORMATION	108
IX.	JEREMIAH AND THE DESTRUCTION OF JERUSALEM	117
X.	THE CAPTIVITY AND THE RESTORATION	124
XI.	THE HELLENISTIC PERIOD	137
XII.	THE HASMONÆANS	146
XIII.	HEROD AND THE ROMANS	163
XIV.	THE RABBINS	184
XV.	THE JEWISH DISPERSION	191

APPENDIX 207

SKETCH OF THE HISTORY

OF

ISRAEL AND JUDAH.

CHAPTER I.

THE BEGINNINGS OF THE NATION.

ACCORDING to the Book of Genesis, Israel was the brother of Edom, and the cousin of Moab and Ammon. These four petty peoples, which may be classed together as the Hebrew group, must at one time have formed some sort of a unity and have passed through a common history which resulted in their settlement in south-eastern Palestine. The Israelites, or rather that section of the Hebrew group which afterwards developed into Israel, appear at first to have been the immediate neighbours of Edom, and to have extended westwards towards the border of Egypt. As regards the ethnological position of the Hebrews as a whole, tradition has it that they had connections not only with the Aramæans of

Osrhoene (Nahor), but also with certain of the old inhabitants of the Sinaitic peninsula (Kenites, Amalek, Midian). To the Canaanites, whose language they had adopted, their relation was that of foreign conquerors and lords to a subject race, (Gen. ix. 26).[1]

Some fifteen centuries before our era a section of the Hebrew group left its ancient seat in the extreme south of Palestine to occupy the not distant pasture lands of Egypt (Goshen), where they carried on their old calling, that of shepherds and goatherds. Although settled within the territory of the Pharaohs, and recognising their authority, they continued to retain all their old characteristics —their language, their patriarchal institutions, their nomad habits of life.

But in course of time these foreign guests were subjected to changed treatment. Forced labour was exacted of them for the construction of new public works in Goshen, an exaction which was felt to be an assault upon their freedom and honour, and which in point of fact was fitted to take away all that was distinctive of their nationality. But they had no remedy at hand, and had submitted in despair, until Moses at last saw a favourable opportunity of deliverance. Reminding his oppressed brethren of the God of their fathers, and urging that their

[1] Comp. Wellhausen, *Die Composition des Hexateuchs und der histor. Bücher* (Berlin, 1889), p. 342 *sqq*.

cause was His, he taught them to regard self-assertion against the Egyptians as an article of religion; and they became united by the determination to seek refuge from oppression in the wilderness which was the dwelling-place of their kindred and the seat of their God. At a time when Egypt was scourged by a grievous plague, the Hebrews broke up their settlement in Goshen one night in spring, and directed their steps towards their old home again. According to the accounts, the king had consented to the exodus, and latterly had even forced it on, but it was none the less a secret flight.

To a not very numerous pastoral people such an undertaking presented no great difficulty. Nevertheless its execution was not to be carried out unimpeded. The Hebrews, compelled to abandon the direct eastward road (Exod. xiii. 17, 18), turned towards the south-west and encamped at last on the Egyptian shore of the northern arm of the Red Sea, where they were overtaken by Pharaoh's army. The situation was a critical one; but a high wind during the night left the shallow sea so low that it became possible to ford it. Moses eagerly accepted the suggestion, and made the venture with success. The Egyptians, rushing after, came up with them on the further shore, and a struggle ensued. But the assailants fought at a disadvantage, the ground being ill-suited for their chariots and horsemen; they fell into confusion and attempted a retreat. Meanwhile the wind had changed; the waters returned, and the pursuers were annihilated.[1]

After turning aside to visit Sinai, as related in Exodus, the emigrants settled at Kadesh, eastwards from Goshen, on the southern borders of Palestine,[2] where they remained for many years, having at the well of Kadesh their sanctuary and judgment-seat only, while with their flocks they ranged over an extensive tract. In all probability their stay at Kadesh was no involuntary detention; rather was it this locality they had immediately had in view in setting out. For a civilised community of from two to three millions such a settlement would, of course, have been impossible; but it was quite sufficient for the immediate requirements of the Goshen shepherds, few in number as they were and inured to the life of the desert. That attempts may have been made by them to obtain possession of the more fertile

---

[1] Exod. xvi. 21, 24, 25, 27, 30, 31. According to the Old Testament the exodus took place 480 years before the building of Solomon's temple, and 960 years before the end of the Babylonian captivity. These figures are "systematic" or at least systematised, but even so they are certainly more trustworthy than the combinations of the Egyptologists.

[2] The site of Sinai (= Horeb ?) hardly admits of ascertainment. The best datum would be the sanctuary of Jethro, if we could identify it with Midian (*Jakut* iv. 451), which lies on the Arabian coast of the Red Sea, obliquely facing the traditional Sinai. With regard to Kadesh, see *Quarterly Statement* of the Palestine Exploration Fund (1871), pp. 20, 21.

country to the north is very likely; but that from
the outset they contemplated the conquest of the
whole of Palestine proper, and that it was only in
expiation of a fault that they were held back at the
gate of the promised land until the whole generation
of the disobedient had died out, is not historically
probable.

We can assign a definite reason for their final
departure from Kadesh. In the district to the east
of Jordan the (Canaanite) Amorites had, sometime
previously, driven the Ammonites from the lower
Jabbok and deprived the Moabites of all their territory to the north of the Arnon; on the plateau
opposite Jericho Heshbon had become the capital of
Sihon, the Amorite king. This sovereign now set
himself to subdue southern Moab also, and not
without success. From these straits the Moabites
were rescued by their cousins, the nomads of the
wilderness of Kadesh. The Israelites came forward
on behalf of what was at once the common Hebrew
cause and their own particular interest; they took
the field against the Amorites, vanquished them in
battle, and broke up the kingdom of Sihon. The
consequence was that the land to the south of the
Arnon remained in the undisputed possession of
Moab, while the victors themselves became masters
of the territory immediately to the north. Settled
thus between Moab and Ammon their kinsmen, the
Israelites supplied the link that was wanting in the

chain of petty Hebrew nationalities established in the south of eastern Palestine.[1]

The army that went out against the Amorites from Kadesh was certainly not exclusively composed of men who, or whose fathers, had accomplished the passage of the Red Sea. Israel was not a formed nation when it left Egypt; and throughout the whole period of its sojourn in the wilderness it continued to be in process of growth. Instead of excluding the kindred elements which offered themselves to it on its new soil, it received and assimilated them. The life they had lived together under Moses had been the first thing to awaken a feeling of solidarity among the tribes which afterwards constituted the nation; whether they had previously been a unity in any sense of the word is doubtful. On the other hand, the basis of the unification of the tribes must certainly have been laid before the conquest of Palestine proper; for with that it broke up, though the memory of it continued. At the same time it must not be supposed that all the twelve tribes already existed side by side in Kadesh. The sons of the concubines of Jacob—Dan and Naphtali, Gad and Asher—manifestly do not pertain to Israel in the same sense as do those of Leah and Rachel; probably they were late arrivals and of very mixed origin. We know, besides, that Benjamin was not born until afterwards,

[1] Wellhausen, l. l., p. 343, *sqq.*

in Palestine. If this view be correct, Israel at first consisted of seven tribes, of which one only, that of Joseph, traced its descent to Rachel, though in point of numbers and physical strength it was the equal of all the others together, while in intellectual force it surpassed them. The remaining six were the sons of Leah:—Reuben, Simeon, Levi, Judah; Issachar, Zebulon. They are always enumerated in this order; the fact that the last two are also invariably mentioned apart from the rest and after Joseph has its explanation in geographical considerations.

The time of Moses is invariably regarded as the properly creative period in Israel's history, and on that account also as giving the pattern and norm for the ages which followed. Indeed, the history of Israel must be held to have begun then, and the foundations of a new epoch to have been laid. The prophets who came after gave, it is true, greater distinctness to the peculiar character of the nation, but they did not make it; on the contrary, it made them. Again, it is true that the movement which resulted in the establishment of the monarchy brought together for the first time into organic unity the elements which previously had existed only in an isolated condition; but Israel's sense of national personality was a thing of much earlier origin, which even in the time of the judges bound the various tribes and families together, and must have had a great hold on the mind of the nation, although there was no formal and binding constitution to give it support. When the Israelites settled in Palestine they found it inhabited by a population superior to themselves both in numbers and in civilisation, which they did not extirpate, but, on the contrary, gradually subdued and absorbed. The process was favoured by affinity of race and similarity of speech; but, however far it went, it never had the effect of making Israelites Canaanites; on the contrary, it made Canaanites Israelites. Notwithstanding their inferiority, numerical and otherwise, they maintained their individuality, and that without the support of any external organisation. Thus a certain inner unity actually subsisted long before it had found any outward political expression; it goes back to the time of Moses, who is to be regarded as its author.

The foundation upon which, at all periods, Israel's sense of its national unity rested was religious in its character. It was the faith which may be summed up in the formula: Jehovah is the God of Israel, and Israel is the people of Jehovah. Moses was not the first discoverer of this faith, but it was through him that it came to be the fundamental basis of the national existence and history.[1] The exigencies of

---

[1] Jehovah is to be regarded as having originally been a family or tribal god, either of the family to which Moses belonged or of the tribe of Joseph, in the possession of which we find the ark of Jehovah, and within which occurs the earliest certain instance of a composite proper name with the word Jehovah for one of its

their position severed a number of kindred clans from their customary surroundings, and drove them into his arms. He undertook the responsibilities of their leader, and the confidence of success which he manifested was justified by the result. But it was not through any merit of his that the undertaking (of which he was the soul) prospered as it did; his design was aided in a wholly unlooked-for way, by a marvellous occurrence quite beyond his control, and which no sagacity could possibly have foreseen. One whom the wind and sea obeyed had given him His aid. Behind him stood One higher than he, whose spirit wrought in him and whose arm wrought for him,—not for his personal aggrandisement indeed, but for the weal of the nation. It was Jehovah. Alike what was done by the deliberate purpose of Moses, and what was done without any human contrivance by nature and by accident, came to be regarded in one great totality as the doing of Jehovah for Israel. Jehovah it was who had directed each step in that process through which these so diverse elements, brought together by the pressure of necessity, had been caused to pass, and in the course of which the first beginnings of a feeling of national unity had been made to grow.

elements (Jeho-shua, Joshua). No essential distinction was felt to exist between Jehovah and El, any more than between Asshur and El; Jehovah was only a special name of El which had become current within a powerful circle, and which on that account was all the more fitted to become the designation of a national god.

This feeling Moses was the first to elicit; he it was also who maintained it in life and cherished its growth. The extraordinary set of circumstances which had first occasioned the new national movement continued to subsist, though in a less degree, throughout the sojourn of the people in the wilderness, and it was under their pressure that Israel continued to be moulded. To Moses, who had been the means of so brilliantly helping out of their first straits the Hebrews who had accompanied him out of Egypt, they naturally turned in all subsequent difficulties; before him they brought all affairs with which they were not themselves able to cope. The authority which his antecedents had secured for him made him, as matter of course, the great national "Kadhi" in the wilderness. Equally as matter of course did he exercise his judicial functions, neither in his own interest nor in his own name, but in the interest of the whole community and in the name of Jehovah. By connecting them with the sanctuary of Jehovah, which stood at the well of Kadesh, he made these functions independent of his person, and thus he laid a firm basis for a consuetudinary law, and became the originator of the Torah in Israel. In doing this he succeeded in inspiring the national being with that which was the very life of his own soul; through the Torah he gave a definite positive expression to their sense of nationality and their idea of God. Jehovah was not merely the God of

Israel; as such he was the God at once of law and of justice, the basis, the informing principle, and the implied postulate of their national consciousness.

The relationship was carried on in precisely the same manner as that in which it had been begun. It was most especially in the graver moments of its history that Israel awoke to full consciousness of itself and of Jehovah. Now, at that time and for centuries afterwards, the highwater marks of history were indicated by the wars it recorded. The name "Israel" means "El does battle," and Jehovah was the warrior El, after whom the nation styled itself. The camp was, so to speak, at once the cradle in which the nation was nursed and the smithy in which it was welded into unity; it was also the primitive sanctuary. There Israel was, and there was Jehovah. If in times of peace the relations between the two had become dormant, they were at once called forth into fullest activity when the alarm of danger was raised; Israel's awakening was always preceded by the awakening of Jehovah. Jehovah awakened men who, under the guidance of His Spirit, placed themselves at the nation's head; in them his proper leadership was visibly expressed. Jehovah went forth with the host to battle, and in its enthusiasm His presence was seen (Judg. v. 13, 23). With signs and wonders from heaven Jehovah decided the struggle carried on upon earth. In it He was always upon Israel's side; on Israel was His whole interest concentrated, although His power (for He was God) reached far beyond their local limits.

Thus Jehovah was in a very real sense a living God; but the manifestations of His life in the great crises of His people's history were of necessity separated by considerable intervals of time. His activity had something abrupt and tumultuary about it, better suited for extraordinary occasions than for ordinary daily life. Traces of this feeling appear very prominently in the later stages of the development. But although the relations between Israel and Israel's God came most strongly into prominence in times of excitement, yet it did not altogether die out in the periods of comparative repose. It was in the case of Jehovah just as in the case of the human leaders of the people, who did not in times of peace wholly lose the influence they had gained in war. Jehovah had His permanent court at the places of worship where in times of quietude men clung to Him that they might not lose Him in times of trouble. His chief, perhaps in the time of Moses His only, sanctuary was with the so-called ark of the covenant. It was a standard, adapted primarily to the requirements of a wandering and warlike life; brought back from the field, it became, as symbol of Jehovah's presence, the central seat of His worship. The cultus itself was more than a mere paying of court to Jehovah, more than a mere expedient for retaining His sympathies against times of necessity; the Torah of Jehovah, the holy administration of law, was conjoined with it. This had first of all been exercised, at the instance of the priest of Midian, by Moses at the well of Kadesh; it was continued after him, at the sanctuary, within the circle of those who had attached themselves to him and were spiritually his heirs. In cases where the wisdom or the competency of the ordinary judges failed, men turned direct to the Godhead, *i.e.*, to the sanctuary and those who served it. Their decisions, whether given according to their own lights or by lot (according to the character of the question) were not derived from any law, but were received direct from Jehovah.[1] The execution of their decisions did not lie with them; they could only advise and teach. Their authority was divine, or, as we should say, moral, in its character; it rested upon that spontaneous recognition of the idea of right which, though unexpressed, was alive and working among the tribes —upon Jehovah Himself, who was the author of this generally diffused sense of right, but revealed the proper determinations on points of detail only to certain individuals. The priestly Torah was an entirely unpolitical or rather prepolitical institution;

---

[1] They were consulted chiefly on points of law, but also on all sorts of difficulties as to what was right and to be done, or wrong and to be avoided.

it had an existence before the state had, and it was one of the invisible foundation pillars on which the state rested.

War and the administration of justice were regarded as matters of religion before they became matters of obligation and civil order; this is all that is really meant when a theocracy is spoken of. Moses certainly organised no formal state, endowed with specific holiness, upon the basis of the proposition "Jehovah is the God of Israel;" or, at all events, if he did so, the fact had not in the slightest degree any practical consequence or historical significance. The old patriarchal system of families and clans continued as before to be the ordinary constitution, if one can apply such a word as constitution at all to an unorganised conglomeration of homogeneous elements. What there was of permanent official authority lay in the hands of the elders and heads of houses; in time of war they commanded each his own household force, and in peace they dispensed justice each within his own circle. But this obviously imperfect and inefficient form of government showed a growing tendency to break down just in proportion to the magnitude of the tasks which the nation in the course of its history was called upon to undertake. Appeal to Jehovah was always in these circumstances resorted to; His court was properly that of last resort, but the ordinary authorities were so inadequate that it had often enough to be applied to. Theocracy, if one may so say, arose as the complement of anarchy. Actual and legal existence (in the modern sense) was predicable only of each of the many clans; the unity of the nation began to be realised through its religion. It was out of the religion of Israel that the commonwealth of Israel unfolded itself —not a *holy* state, but *the* state. And the state continued to be, consciously, rooted in religion, which prevented it from quitting or losing its *rapport* with the soil from which it had originally sprung. With the intermediate and higher stages of political organisation, with the building of the upper structure, however, religion had no concern; they were too far removed from the foundation. The derivative, which did not carry immediately in itself its own title to exist, was a matter of indifference to it; what had come into being it suffered to go its own way as soon as it was capable of asserting its independence. For this reason it always turned by preference to the future, not in a utopian but in a thoroughly practical way; by a single step only did it keep ahead of the present. It prepared the way for such developments as are not derived from existing institutions, but spring immediately from the depths in which human society has its secret and mysterious roots.

The expression "Jehovah is the God of Israel," accordingly, meant that every task of the nation, internal as well as external, was conceived as holy. It certainly did not mean that the almighty Creator of heaven and earth was conceived of as having first made a covenant with this one people that by them He might be truly known and worshipped. It was not as if Jehovah had originally been regarded as the God of the universe who subsequently became the God of Israel; on the contrary, He was primarily Israel's God, and only afterwards (very long afterwards) did He come to be regarded as the God of the universe. For Moses to have given to the Israelites an "enlightened conception of God" would have been to have given them a stone instead of bread; it is in the highest degree probable that, with regard to the essential nature of Jehovah, as distinct from His relation to men, he allowed them to continue in the same way of thinking with their fathers. With theoretical truths, which were not at all in demand, he did not occupy himself, but purely with practical questions which were put and urged by the pressure of the times. The religious starting-point of the history of Israel was remarkable, not for its novelty, but for its normal character. In all ancient primitive peoples the relation in which God is conceived to stand to the circumstances of the nation—in other words, religion—furnishes a motive for law and morals; in the case of none did it become so with such purity and power as in that of the Israelites.

Whatever Jehovah may have been conceived to be in His essential nature—God of the thunderstorm or the like—this fell more and more into the background as mysterious and transcendental; the subject was not one for inquiry. All stress was laid upon His activity within the world of mankind, whose ends He made one with His own. Religion thus did not make men partakers in a divine life, but contrariwise it made God a partaker in the life of men; life in this way was not straitened by it, but enlarged. The so-called "particularism" of Israel's idea of God was in fact the real strength of Israel's religion; it thus escaped from barren mythologisings, and became free to apply itself to the moral tasks which are always given, and admit of being discharged, only in definite spheres. As God of the nation, Jehovah became the God of justice and of right; as God of justice and right, He came to be thought of as the highest, and at last as the only, power in heaven and earth.

(In the preceding sketch the attempt has been made to exhibit Mosaism as it must be supposed to have existed on the assumption that the history of Israel commenced with it, and that for centuries it continued to be the ideal root out of which that history continued to grow. This being assumed, we cannot treat the legislative portion of the Pentateuch as a source from which our knowledge of what Mosaism really was can be derived; for it cannot in any sense be regarded as the starting-point of the subsequent development. If it was the work of Moses, then we must suppose it to have remained a dead letter for centuries, and only through King Josiah and Ezra the scribe to have become operative in the national history.[1] The historical tradition which has reached us relating to the period of the judges and of the kings of Israel is the main source, though only of course in an indirect way, of our knowledge of Mosaism. But within the Pentateuch itself also the *historical* tradition about Moses (which admits of being distinguished, and must carefully be separated, from the *legislative*, although the latter often clothes itself in narrative form) is in its main features manifestly trustworthy, and can only be explained as resting on actual facts.

From the historical tradition, then, it is certain that Moses was the founder of the Torah. But the legislative tradition cannot tell us what were the positive contents of his Torah. In fact it can be shown that throughout the whole of the older period the Torah was no finished legislative code, but consisted entirely of the oral decisions and instructions of the priests; as a whole it was potential only; what actually existed were the individual sentences given by the priesthood as they were asked for. Thus Moses was not regarded as the promulgator

[1] Comp. chaps. viii. and x.

once for all of a national constitution, but rather as the first to call into activity the actual sense for law and justice, and to begin the series of oral decisions which were continued after him by the priests. He was the founder of the nation out of which the Torah and prophecy came as later growths. He laid the basis of Israel's subsequent peculiar individuality, not by any one formal act, but in virtue of his having throughout the whole of his long life been the people's leader, judge, and centre of union.

A correct conception of the manner in which the Torah was made by him can be derived from the narrative contained in Exod. xviii., but not from the long section which follows, relating to the Sinaitic covenant (chap. xix. *seq.*). The giving of the law at Sinai has only a formal, not to say dramatic, significance. It is the product of the poetic necessity for such a representation of the manner in which the people was constituted Jehovah's people as should appeal directly and graphically to the imagination. Only so can we justly interpret those expressions according to which Jehovah with His own mouth thundered the ten commandments down from the mountain to the people below, and afterwards for forty days held a confidential conference with Moses alone on the summit. For the sake of producing a solemn and vivid impression that is represented as having taken place in a single thrilling moment, which in reality occurred slowly and almost unobserved. Why Sinai should have been chosen as the scene admits of ready explanation. It was the Olympus of the Hebrew peoples, the earthly seat of the Godhead, and as such it continued to be regarded by the Israelites even after their settlement in Palestine (Judg. v. 4, 5). This immemorial sanctity of Sinai it was that led to its being selected as the ideal scene of the giving of the law, not conversely. If we eliminate from the historical narrative the long Sinaitic section which has but a loose connection with it, the wilderness of Kadesh becomes the locality of the preceding and subsequent events. It was during the sojourn of many years here that the organisation of the nation, in any historical sense, took place. "There He made for them statute and ordinance, and there He proved them," as we read in Exod. xv. 25 in a dislocated poetical fragment. "Judgment and trial," "Massa and Meribah," point to Kadesh as the place referred to; there at all events is the scene of the narrative immediately following (Exod. xvii. = Num. xx.), and doubtless also of Exod. xviii.

If the legislation of the Pentateuch cease as a whole to be regarded as an authentic source for our knowledge of what Mosaism was, it becomes a somewhat precarious matter to make any exception in favour of the Decalogue. In particular, the following arguments against its authenticity must be taken into account:—(1) According to Exod. xxxiv. the commandments which stood upon the two tables were quite different. (2) The prohibition of images was during the older period quite unknown; Moses himself is said to have made a brazen serpent which, down to Hezekiah's time, continued to be worshipped at Jerusalem as an image of Jehovah. (3) The essentially and necessarily national character of the older phases of the religion of Jehovah completely disappears in the quite universal code of morals, which is given in the Decalogue as the fundamental law of Israel; but the entire series of religious personalities throughout the period of the judges and the kings—from Deborah, who praised Jael's treacherous act of murder, to David, who treated his prisoners of war with the utmost cruelty—make it very difficult to believe that the religion of Israel was, from the outset, one of a specifically moral character. The true spirit of the old religion may be gathered much more truly from Judg. v. than from Exod. xx. (4) It is extremely doubtful whether the actual monotheism, which is undoubtedly presupposed in the universal moral precepts of the Decalogue, could have formed the foundation of a national religion. It was first developed out of the national religion at the downfall of the nation, and thereupon kept its hold upon the people in an artificial manner by means of the idea of a covenant formed by the God of the universe with, in the first instance, Israel alone.[1]

As for the question regarding the historical presuppositions of Mosaism, there generally underlies it a misunderstanding arising out of theological intellectualism—an attribute found with special frequency among non-theologians. Moses gave no new idea of God to his people. The question whence he could have derived it therefore need not be raised. It could not possibly be worse answered, however, than by a reference to his relations with the priestly caste of Egypt and their wisdom. It is not to be believed that an Egyptian deity could inspire the Hebrews of Goshen with courage for the struggle against the Egyptians, or that an abstraction of esoteric speculation could become the national deity of Israel. It is not inconceivable indeed, although at the same time quite incapable of proof, that Moses was indebted to the Egyptian priests for certain advantages of personal culture, or that he borrowed from them on all hands in external details of organisation or in matters of ritual. But the origin of the germ which developed into Israel is not to be sought for in Egypt, and Jehovah has nothing in common with the colourless divinity of Penta-ur. That monotheism must have been a foreign importation, because it is contrary to that sexual dualism of Godhead which is said to be the

[1] Comp. chaps. vi.-x.

fundamental characteristic of Semitic religion, is an untenable exaggeration which has recently become popular out of opposition to the familiar thesis about the monotheistic instinct of the Semites.[1] Moab, Ammon, and Edom, Israel's nearest kinsfolk and neighbours, were monotheists in precisely the same sense in which Israel itself was; but it would be foolish surely in their case to think of foreign importation.

Manetho's statements about the Israelites are for the most part to be regarded as malicious inventions: whether any genuine tradition underlies them at all is a point much needing to be investigated. The story of Exod. ii. 1 *seq.* is a mythus which recurs elsewhere, to which no further significance is attached, for that Moses was trained in all the wisdom of the Egyptians is vouched for by no earlier authorities than Philo and the New Testament. According to the Old Testament tradition his connection is with Jethro's priesthood or with that of the Kenites. This historical presupposition of Mosaism has external evidence in its favour, and is inherently quite probable.)

[1] Nöldeke, *Literar. Centralbl.*, 1877, p. 365.

CHAPTER II.

THE SETTLEMENT IN PALESTINE.

THE kingdom of Sihon did not permanently suffice the Israelites, and the disintegration of the Canaanites to the west of Jordan in an endless number of kingdoms and cities invited attack. The first essay was made by Judah in conjunction with Simeon and Levi, but was far from prosperous. Simeon and Levi were annihilated; Judah also, though successful in mastering the mountain land to the west of the Dead Sea, was so only at the cost of severe losses which were not again made up until the accession of the Kenite families of the south (Caleb). As a consequence of the secession of these tribes, a new division of the nation into Israel and Judah took the place of that which had previously subsisted between the families of Leah and Rachel; under Israel were included all the tribes except Simeon, Levi, and Judah, which three are no longer mentioned in Judg. v., where all the others are carefully and exhaustively enumerated. This half-abortive first invasion of the west was followed by a second, which was stronger and attended with much better results. It was led by the tribe of Joseph, to which the others attached themselves, Reuben and Gad only remaining behind in the old settlements. The district to the north of Judah, inhabited afterwards by Benjamin, was the first to be attacked. It was not until after several towns of this district had one by one fallen into the hands of the conquerors that the Canaanites set about a united resistance. They were, however, decisively repulsed by Joshua in the neighbourhood of Gibeon; and by this victory the Israelites became masters of the whole central plateau of Palestine. The first camp, at Gilgal, near the ford of Jordan, which had been maintained until then, was now removed, and the ark of Jehovah brought further inland (perhaps by way of Bethel) to Shiloh, where henceforward the headquarters were fixed, in a position which seemed as if it had been expressly made to favour attacks upon the fertile tract lying beneath it on the north. The Bne Rachel now occupied the new territory which up to that time had been acquired—Benjamin, in immediate contiguity with the frontier of Judah, then Ephraim, stretching to beyond Shiloh, and lastly Manasseh, furtherest to the north, as far as to the plain of Jezreel. The centre of gravity, so to speak, already lay in Ephraim, to which belonged Joshua and the ark.

It is mentioned as the last achievement of Joshua

that at the waters of Merom he defeated Jabin, king of Hazor, and the allied princes of Galilee, thereby opening up the north for Israelitish settlers. It is quite what we should expect that a great and united blow had to be struck at the Canaanites of the north before the new-comers could occupy it in peace; and King Jabin, who reappears at a later date, certainly does not suit the situation described in Judg. iv., v.

(The Book of Joshua represents the conquest of western Palestine as having been the common undertaking of all the tribes together, which, after the original inhabitants have been extirpated, are exhibited as laying the ownerless country at Joshua's feet in order that he may divide it by lot amongst them. But this is a "systematic" generalisation, contradicted by the facts which we otherwise know. For we possess another account of the conquest of Palestine, that of Judg. i., which runs parallel with the Book of Joshua. It is shorter indeed and more superficial, yet in its entire mode of presenting the subject more historical. According to its narrative, it appears that Joshua was the leader of Joseph and Benjamin only, with whom indeed Issachar, Zebulon, Dan, Naphtali, and Asher made common cause. But before his time the tribe of Judah had already crossed the Jordan and effected a lodgment in the territory which lay between the earlier seat of the nation in the wilderness of Kadesh and its then settlement on the plateau of Moab, forming in some degree a link of connection between the two. It might be supposed that the tribe of Judah had not taken the longer route to the eastward of the Dead Sea at all, but had already at Kadesh broken off from the main body and thence turned its steps directly northward. But the representation actually given in Judg. i., to the effect that it was from the direction of the Jordan and not from that of the Negeb that they came to take possession of their land, finds its confirmation in the fact that the southern portion of their territory was the last to come into their possession. The tradition is unwavering that Hebron was taken not by Judah but by Caleb, a family which stood in friendly relations with Israel, but had no connection with it by blood. It was only through the policy of David that Caleb, Othniel, Jerachmeel, and the rest of the Kenites who had their homes in the Negeb became completely incorporated with Judah, so that Hebron became at last the capital of that tribe. Its oldest seats, however, lay further to the north, in the region of Tekoa, Bethlehem, Baal-Judah.

It harmonises well with this view to suppose that Simeon and Levi must have made at the same time their attempt to effect a settlement in the hill-country of Ephraim. One of their families, Dinah bat Leah, met with a favourable reception in the town of Shechem, and began to mix freely with its population, and thus the way was paved for the establishment of peaceable relations between the old inhabitants of the land and the new importations. But these relations were brought to an end by the two brothers who, in concert it must be supposed with their sister, fell upon the Shechemites and massacred them. The final result proved disastrous. The Canaanites of the surrounding country united against them and completely destroyed them. There can be no doubt as to the trustworthiness of the somewhat enigmatical records of those events which are given in Gen. xlix. and xxxiv.; in no other way is it possible to explain why Simeon and Levi, which originally came upon the stage of history on an equal footing with Reuben and Judah, should have already disappeared as independent tribes at the very beginning of the period of the judges. Now, that the destruction of Shechem by the Manassite Abimelech is quite distinct from the attack made by Simeon and Levi need hardly be said. On the other hand, the occurrence cannot be regarded as pre-Mosaic, but must be assigned to a time previous to the conquest of the hill-country of Ephraim by Joseph; for after Joseph's settlement there the two sons of Leah had manifestly nothing more to hope for in that locality. We are shut up, therefore, to the conclusion that they crossed the Jordan at the same time as Judah separated himself from the main body in search of a suitable territory. That Simeon accompanied Judah in the first westward attempt is expressly stated in Judg. i. The fate of Levi, again, cannot be separated from that of Simeon (Gen. xlix. 5–7); that he is not expressly mentioned in Judg. i. ought not to cause surprise, when it is considered that later generations which regarded Levi as neither more nor less than a priest would have some difficulty in representing him as a thoroughly secular tribe. Such nevertheless he must have been, for the poet in Gen. xlix. 5–7 puts him on a footing of perfect equality with Simeon, and attributes to both brothers a very secular and bloodthirsty character; he has no conception that Levi has a sacred vocation which is the reason of the dispersion of the tribe; the dispersion, on the contrary, is regarded as a curse and no blessing, an annihilation and not the means of giving permanence to its tribal individuality. The shattered remains of Simeon, and doubtless those of Levi also, became incorporated with Judah, which thenceforward was the sole representative of the three sons of Leah, who according to the genealogy had been born immediately after Reuben the first-born. Judah itself seems at the same time to have suffered severely. Of its three older branches, Er, Onan, and Shelah, one only survived, and only by the accession of foreign elements did the tribe regain its vigour—by the fresh blood which the Kenites of the Negeb brought. For Zarah and Pharez, which took the place of Er and Onan after these had disappeared, belonged originally, not to Israel, but to Hezron or the Kenites; under this designation are included families like those of Othniel, Jerachmeel, and Caleb, and, as has been already remarked, even in David's time these were not reckoned as strictly belonging to Judah. Thus the depletion which the tribe had to suffer in the struggle with the Canaanites at the beginning of the period of the judges was the remote cause of the prominence which, according to 1 Chron. ii., the Bne Hezron afterwards attained in Judah. The survivors of Simeon also appear to have been forced back upon these Hezronites in the Negeb; the cities assigned to them in the Book of Joshua all belong to that region.)

Even after the united resistance of the Canaanites had been broken, each individual community had still enough to do before it could take firm hold of the spot which it had searched out for itself or to which it had been assigned. The business of effecting permanent settlement was just a continuation of the former struggle, only on a diminished scale; every tribe and every family now fought for its own hand after the preliminary work had been accomplished by a united effort. Naturally, therefore, the conquest was at first but an incomplete one. The plain which fringed the coast was hardly touched; so also the valley of Jezreel with its girdle of fortified cities stretching from Acco to Bethshean. All that was subdued in the strict sense of that word was the mountainous land, particularly the southern hill-country of " Mount Ephraim ; " yet, even here the Canaanites retained possession of not a few cities, such as Jebus, Shechem, Thebez. It was only after the lapse of centuries that all the lacunæ were filled up, and the Canaanite enclaves made tributary.

The Israelites had the extraordinarily disintegrated state of the enemy to thank for the ease with which they had achieved success. The first storm subsided comparatively soon, and conquerors and conquered alike learned to accommodate themselves to the new circumstances. Then the Canaanites once more collected all their energies to strike a blow for freedom. Under the hegemony of Sisera a great league was formed, and the plain of Jezreel became the centre of the reorganised power which made itself felt by its attacks both northwards and southwards. The Israelites were strangely helpless; it was as if neither shield nor spear could be found among their 40,000 fighting men. But at last there came an impulse from above, and brought life and soul to the unorganised mass; Deborah sent out the summons to the tribes, Barak came forward as their leader against the kings of Canaan who had assembled under Sisera's command by the brook of Kishon. The cavalry of the enemy was unable to withstand the impetuous rush of the army of Jehovah, and Sisera himself perished in the flight. From that day the Canaanites, although many strong towns continued to be held by them, never again raised their heads.

After these occurrences some further changes of a fundamental character took place in the relations of the tribes. The Danites proved unable to hold against the forward pressure of the Philistines their territory on the coast to the west of Benjamin and Ephraim; they accordingly sought a new settlement, which was found in the north at the foot of Hermon. In this way all the secondary tribes westward of Jordan (Asher, Naphtali, Dan) came to have their seats beside each other in the northern division of the land. Eastward of Jordan, Reuben rapidly fell from his old prominence, sharing the fate of his next eldest brethren Simeon and Levi. When Eglon of Moab took Jericho, and laid Benjamin under tribute, it is obvious that he must previously have made himself master of Reuben's territory. This territory became thenceforward a subject of constant dispute between Moab and Israel; the efforts to recover it, however, did not proceed from Reuben himself, but from Gad, a tribe which knew how to assert itself with vigour against the enemies by which it was surrounded. But if the Hebrews lost ground in the south, they

SETTLEMENT IN PALESTINE.

materially enlarged their borders in the north of the land eastward of Jordan. Various Manassite families, finding their holdings at home too small, crossed the Jordan and founded colonies in Bashan and northern Gilead. Although this colonisation, on account of the rivalry of the Aramæans, who were also pressing forward in this direction, was but imperfectly successful, it nevertheless was of very great importance, inasmuch as it served to give new strength to the bonds that united the eastern with the western tribes. Not only was Gilead not lost; it even became a very vigorous member of the body-politic.[1]

The times of agitation and insecurity which followed upon the conquest of Palestine invited attacks by the eastern nomads, and once more the Israelite peasantry showed all its old helplessness, until at last the indignation of a Manassite of good family, Gideon or Jerubbaal, was roused by the

[1] It is probable that Manasseh's migration to the territory eastward of Jordan took place from the west, and later than the time of Moses. The older portions of the Hexateuch speak not of two and a half but only of two trans-Jordanic tribes, and exclude Manasseh; according to them the kingdom of Sihon alone was subdued by Moses, not that of Og also, the latter, indeed, being a wholly legendary personage. In the song of Deborah, Machir is reckoned among the western tribes, and it was not until much later that this became the designation of the Manassites eastward of Jordan. It is also worth noticing that Jair's colonisation of northern Gilead did not take place until the time of the judges (Judg. x. 3, *sqq.*), but is related also in Num. xxxii. 39–42.

Midianites, who had captured some of his brothers and put them to death. With his family, that of Abiezer, he gave pursuit, and, overtaking the enemy on the borders of the wilderness, inflicted on them such chastisement as put an end to these incursions. His heroism had consequences which reached far beyond the scope of his original purpose. He became the champion of the peasantry against the freebooters, of the cultivated land against the waste; social respect and predominance were his rewards. In his native town of Ophrah he kept up a great establishment, where also he built a temple with an image of Jehovah overlaid with the gold which he had taken from the Midianites. He transmitted to his sons an authority, which was not limited to Abiezer and Manasseh alone, but, however slightly and indirectly, extended over Ephraim as well.

On the foundations laid by Gideon Abimelech his son sought to establish a kingship over Israel, that is, over Ephraim and Manasseh. The predominance, however, which had been naturally accorded to his father in virtue of his personal merits, Abimelech looked upon as a thing seized by force and to be maintained with injustice; and in this way he soon destroyed those fair beginnings out of which even at that time a kingdom might have arisen within the house of Joseph. The one permanent fruit of his activity was that Shechem

SETTLEMENT IN PALESTINE.

was destroyed as a Canaanite city and rebuilt for Israel.[1]

The most important change of the period of the judges went on gradually and in silence. The old population of the country, which, according to Deuteronomy, was to have been exterminated, slowly became amalgamated with the new. In this way the Israelites received a very important accession to their numbers. In Deborah's time the fighting men of Israel numbered 40,000; the tribe of Dan, when it migrated to Laish, counted 600 warriors; Gideon pursued the Midianites with 300. But in the reigns of Saul and David we find a population reckoned by millions. The rapid increase is to be accounted for by the incorporation of the Canaanites.

At the same time the Hebrews learned to participate in the culture of the Canaanites, and quietly entered into the enjoyment of the labours of their predecessors. From the pastoral they advanced to the agricultural stage; corn and wine, the olive and the fig, with them are habitually spoken of as the necessaries of life. It was not strange that this change in the manner of their everyday life should be attended with certain consequences in the sphere of religion also. It is inconceivable that the Is-

[1] On the narratives contained in the Book of Judges see Wellhausen, l. l. p. 215 *sqq.*; especially on Barak and Sisera, p. 220 *sqq.*; on Gideon and Abimelech, p. 223, *sqq.*, p. 353, *sqq.*; on Jephthah, Samson, the Danite migration, and the Benjamites of Gibeah, pp. 228-238.

raelites should have brought with them out of the desert the cultus they observed in the time of the kings (Exod. xxii. xxiii. xxiv.), which throughout presupposed the fields and gardens of Palestine; they borrowed it from the Canaanites.[1] This is confirmed by the fact that they took over from these the "Bamoth" or "high places" also, notwithstanding the prohibition in Deut. xii.

It was natural enough that the Hebrews should also appropriate the divinity worshipped by the Canaanite peasants as the giver of their corn, wine, and oil, the Baal whom the Greeks identified with Dionysus. The apostasy to Baal, on the part of the first generation which had quitted the wilderness and adopted a settled agricultural life, is attested alike by historical and prophetical tradition. Doubtless Baal, as the god of the land of Canaan, and Jehovah, as the God of the nation of Israel, were in the first instance co-ordinated.[2] But it was not to be expected that the divinity of the land should permanently be different from the God of the dominant people. In proportion as Israel identified itself with the conquered territory, the divinities also were identified. Hence arose a certain syncretism

---

[1] In the earliest case where the feast of the ingathering, afterwards the chief feast of the Israelites, is mentioned, it is celebrated by Canaanites of Shechem in honour of Baal (Judg. ix. 27).

[2] In Judges v. Jehovah retains his original abode in the wilderness of Sinai, and only on occasions of necessity quits it to come to Palestine.

between Baal and Jehovah, which had not been got over even in the time of the prophet Hosea. At the same time the functions of Baal were more frequently transferred to Jehovah than conversely. Canaan and Baal represented the female, Israel and Jehovah the male, part in this union.

Had the Israelites remained in the wilderness and in barbarism, the historical development they subsequently reached would hardly have been possible; their career would have been like that of Amalek, or, at best, like those of Edom, Moab, and Ammon. Their acceptance of civilisation was undoubtedly a step in the forward direction, but as certainly did it also involve a peril. It involved an overloading, as it were, of the system with materials which it was incapable of assimilating at once. The material tasks imposed threatened to destroy the religious basis of the old national life. The offensive and defensive alliances among the tribes gradually dissolved under the continuance of peace; the subsequent occupation of the country dispersed those whom the camp had united. The enthusiastic *élan* with which the conquest had been achieved gave way to the petty drudgery by which the individual families, each in its own circle, had to accommodate themselves to their new surroundings. Yet under the ashes the embers were still aglow; and the course of history ever fanned them anew into flame, bringing home to Israel the truths that man does not live by bread alone, and that there are other things of worth than those which Baal can bestow; it brought ever again into the foreground the divineness of heroical self-sacrifice of the individual for the good of the nation.

CHAPTER III.

THE FOUNDATION OF THE KINGDOM, AND THE FIRST THREE KINGS.

THE Philistines were the means of arousing from their slumber Israel and Jehovah. From their settlements by the sea on the low-lying plain which skirts the mountains of Judah on the west, they pressed northwards into the plain of Sharon, and thence into the plain of Jezreel beyond, which is connected with that of Sharon by the upland valley of Dothan. Here, having driven out the Danites, they came into direct contact with the tribe of Joseph, the chief bulwark of Israel, and a great battle took place at Aphek, where the plain of Sharon merges into the valley of Dothan. The Philistines were victorious, and carried off as a trophy the Israelite standard, the ark of Jehovah. Their further conquests included, not only the plain of Jezreel and the hill country bordering it on the south, but also the proper citadel of the country, "Mount Ephraim." The old sanctuary at Shiloh was destroyed by them; its temple of Jehovah thenceforward lay in ruins. Their supremacy extended as far as to Benjamin; the Philistines had a *neçib* in Gibeah.1 But the assertion that they had confiscated all weapons and removed all smiths must be regarded as an unhistorical exaggeration; under their *régime* at all events it was possible for the messengers of a beleaguered city on the east of Jordan to summon their countrymen in the west to their relief.

The shame of the Israelites under the reproach of Philistine oppression, led, in the first instance, to a widespread exaltation of religious feeling. Troops of ecstatic enthusiasts showed themselves here and there, and went about with musical accompaniments in processions, which often took the shape of wild dances; even men of the most sedate temperament were sometimes smitten with the contagion, and drawn into the charmed circle. In such a phenomenon occurring in the East, there was nothing intrinsically strange; among the Canaanites such "Nebiim"—for so they were styled—had long been familiar, and they continued to exist in the country, after the old fashion, long after their original char-

---

[1] *Neçib* is an Aramaic word of uncertain meaning. In the name of the town Neçibin (Nisibis) it certainly seems to mean "pillars;" according to 1 Kings iv. 5 and xxii. 48 [A.V. 47] (where it is pointed *niççab*), "governor" seems the best translation, and this is the only rendering consistent with the expression in 1 Sam. xiii. 3 ("Jonathan slew the *neçib*," &c.).

acter, so far as Israel was concerned, had been wholly lost. The new thing at this juncture was that this spirit passed over upon Israel, and that the best members of the community were seized by it. It afforded an outlet for the suppressed excitement of the nation.

The new-kindled zeal had for its object not the abolition of Baal worship, but resistance to the enemies of Israel. Religion and patriotism were then identical. This spirit of the times was understood by an old man, Samuel ben Elkanah, who lived at Ramah, in south-western Ephraim. He was not himself one of the Nebiim; on the contrary, he was a seer of that old type which had for a long time existed amongst the Hebrews much as we find it amongst the Greeks or Arabs. Raised by his foreseeing talent to a position of great prominence, he found opportunity to occupy himself with other questions besides those which he was professionally called on to answer. The national distress weighed upon his heart; the neighbouring peoples had taught him to recognise the advantages which are secured by the consolidation of families and tribes into a kingdom. But Samuel's peculiar merit lay, not in discovering what it was that the nation needed, but in finding out the man who was capable of supplying that need. Having come to know Saul ben Kish, a Benjamite of the town of Gibeah, a man of gigantic form, and swift, enthusiastic nature, he declared to him his destiny to become king over Israel.

Saul very soon had an opportunity for showing whether Samuel had been a true seer or no. The city of Jabesh in Gilead was besieged by the Ammonites, and the inhabitants declared themselves ready to surrender should they fail in obtaining speedy succour from their countrymen. Their messengers had passed through all Israel without meeting with anything more helpful than pity, until at last tidings of their case reached Saul as he was returning with a yoke of oxen from the field. Hewing his cattle in pieces, he caused the portions to be sent in all directions, with the threat that so should it be done with the oxen of every one who should refuse to help in relieving Jabesh. The people obeyed the summons, fell suddenly one morning upon the Ammonites, and delivered the beleaguered city.

Having thus found Saul the man for their need, they refused to let him go. In Gilgal, Joshua's old camp, they anointed him king. The act was equivalent to imposing upon him the conduct of the struggle against the Philistines, and so he understood it. The first signal for the attack was given by his son Jonathan, when he slew the *neçib* of the Philistines at Gibeah. These, in consequence, advanced in force towards the focus of the revolt, and took up a position opposite Gibeah on the north, being divided from it only by the gorge of Michmash. Only a few hundred Benjamites ventured to remain with Saul. The struggle opened with a piece of genuine old heroic daring. While the Philistines were dispersed over the country in foraging expeditions, Jonathan, accompanied by his armour-bearer only, and without the knowledge of Saul, made an attack upon the weak post which they had left behind at the pass of Michmash. After the first had been surprised and overmastered, the others took to flight, no doubt in the belief that the two assailants were supported. They carried their panic with them into the half-deserted camp, whence it spread among the various foraging bands. The commotion was observed from Gibeah opposite, and, without pausing to consult the priestly oracle, King Saul determined to attack the camp. The attempt was completely successful, but involved no more than the camp and its stores; the Philistines themselves effected an unmolested retreat by the difficult road of Bethhoron.

Saul was no mere raw stripling when he ascended the throne; he already had a grown-up son at his side. Nor was he of insignificant descent, the family to which he belonged being a widespread one, and his heritage considerable. His establishment at Gibeah was throughout his entire reign the nucleus of his kingdom. The men on whom he could always reckon were his Benjamite kinsmen. He recognised as belonging to him no other public function besides that of war; the internal affairs of the country he permitted to remain as they had been before his accession. War was at once the business and the resource of the new kingdom. It was carried on against the Philistines without interruption, though for the most part not in the grand style, but rather in a series of border skirmishes.[1]

It is not without significance that the warlike revival of the nation proceeded from Benjamin. By the battle of Aphek Ephraim had lost at once the hegemony and its symbols (the camp-sanctuary at Shiloh, the ark of the covenant). The centre of Israel gravitated southward, and Benjamin became the connecting-link between Ephraim and Judah. It would appear that there the tyranny of the Philistines was not so much felt. Their attacks never were made through Judah, but always came from the north; on the other hand, people fled from them southwards, as is instanced by the priests of Shiloh, who settled in Nob, near Jerusalem. Through Saul Judah entered definitely into the history of Israel; it belonged to his kingdom, and

---

[1] As regards the position of Samuel in the theocracy and the relation in which he stood to Saul, the several narratives in the Book of Samuel differ widely. The preceding account, so far as it relates to Samuel, is based upon 1 Sam. ix., x. 1-15, xi., where he appears simply as a Rôeh at Ramah, and has nothing to do either with the administration of the theocracy or with the Nebiim. Compare Wellhausen, l. l. p. 243 *sqq*.

it more than most others supplied him with energetic and faithful supporters. His famous expedition against the Amalekites had been undertaken purely in the interests of Judah, for it only could possibly suffer from their marauding hordes.

Among the men of Judah whom the war brought to Gibeah, David ben Jesse of Bethlehem took a conspicuous place; his skill on the harp brought him into close relations with the king. He became Saul's armour-bearer, afterwards the most intimate friend of his son, finally the husband of his daughter. While he was thus winning the affections of the court, he at the same time became the declared favourite of the people, the more so because unexampled good fortune attended him in all he undertook. This excited the jealousy of Saul, naturally enough in an age in which the king always required to be the best man. Its first outburst admitted of explanation as occasioned by an attack of illness; but soon it became obtrusively clear that the king's love for his son-in-law had changed into bitter hatred. Jonathan warned his friend and facilitated his flight, the priests of Nob at the same time providing him with arms and food. He went into the wilderness of Judah, and became the leader of a miscellaneous band of outlaws who had been attracted by his name to lead a roving life under his leadership. His kinsmen from Bethlehem were of their number, but also Philistines and Hittites.

Out of this band David's bodyguard subsequently grew, the nucleus of his army. They reckoned also a priest among them, Abiathar ben Ahimelech ben Ahitub ben Phinehas ben Eli, the solitary survivor of the massacre of the sons of Eli at Nob which Saul had ordered on account of suspected conspiracy with David. Through him David was able to have recourse to the sacred lot before the ephod. In the end he found it impossible to hold his own in Judah against Saul's persecutions, especially as his countrymen for the most part withheld their assistance. He therefore took the desperate step of placing his services at the disposal of Achish the Philistine king of Gath, by whom he was received with open arms, the town of Ziklag being assigned him as a residence. Here with his band he continued to follow his old manner of life as an independent prince, subject only to an obligation to render military service to Achish.

Meanwhile the Philistines had once more mustered their forces and marched by the usual route against Israel. Saul did not allow them to advance upon Gibeah, but awaited their attack in the plain of Jezreel. A disastrous battle on Mount Gilboa ensued; after seeing his three eldest sons fall one after another at his side, Saul threw himself upon his sword, and was followed by his armour-bearer. The defeat seemed to have undone the work of his life. The immediate consequence at least was that the Philistines regained their lost ascendency over the country to the west of Jordan. Beyond Jordan, however, Abner, the cousin and generalissimo of Saul, made his son Ishbaal, still a minor, king in Mahanaim, and he was successful in again establishing the dominion of the house over Jezreel, Ephraim, and Benjamin, of course in uninterrupted struggle with the Philistines.

But he did not regain hold of Judah. David seized the opportunity to set up for himself, with the sanction of the Philistines, and, it may safely be presumed, as their vassal, a separate principality which had its centre of gravity in the south, which was inhabited, not by the tribe of Judah properly so called, but by the Calebites and Jerachmeelites. This territory Abner disputed with him in vain. In the protracted feud between the houses of Saul and David, the fortunes of war declared themselves ever increasingly for the latter. Personal causes at last brought matters to a crisis. Abner, by taking to himself a concubine of Saul's called Rizpah, had roused Ishbaal's suspicions that he was aiming at the inheritance, and was challenged on the point. This proved too much for his patience, and forthwith he abandoned the cause of his ward (the hopelessness of which had already perhaps become apparent), and entered into negotiations with David at Hebron. When about to set out on his return he fell by the hand of Joab in the gate of Hebron, a victim of jealousy and blood-feud. His plans nevertheless were realised. His death left Israel leaderless and in great confusion; Ishbaal was personally insignificant, and the people's homage continued to be rendered to him only out of grateful fidelity to his father's memory. At this juncture he also fell by assassins' hands. As he was taking his midday rest, and even the portress had gone to sleep over her task of cleaning wheat, two Benjamite captains introduced themselves into his palace at Mahanaim and murdered him in the vain hope of earning David's thanks. The elders of Israel no longer hesitated about offering David the crown, which he accepted.

His residence was immediately transferred from Hebron to Jebus, which until then had remained in possession of the Canaanites, and first derives historical importance from him. It lay on the border between Israel and Judah,—still within the territory of Benjamin, but not far from Bethlehem; near also to Nob, the old priestly city. David made it not only the political but also the religious metropolis by transferring thither from Kirjath-jearim the ark of the covenant, which he placed within his citadel on what afterwards became the temple hill.

Still the crown was far from being a merely honorary possession; it involved heavy responsibilities, and doubtless what contributed more than anything else to David's elevation to the throne was the general recognition of the fact that he was the man best fitted on the whole to overtake the labour it brought with it, viz., the prosecution of the war with the Philistines, a war which was as it were the forge in which the kingdom of Israel was welded into one. The struggle began with the transference of the seat of royalty to Jerusalem; unfortunately we possess only scanty details as to its progress, hardly anything more indeed than a few anecdotes about deeds of prowess by individual heroes. The result was in the end that David completed what Saul had begun, and broke for ever the Philistine yoke. This was undoubtedly the greatest achievement of his reign.

From the defensive against the Philistines David proceeded to aggressive war, in which he subjugated the three kinsfolk of Israel—Moab, Ammon, and Edom. He appears to have come into conflict first with the Moabites, whom he vanquished and treated with savage atrocity. Not long afterwards the king of Ammon died, and David sent an embassy of condolence to Hanun his successor. Hanun suspected in this a sinister design,—a suspicion we can readily understand if David had already, as is probable, subjugated Moab,—and with the utmost contumely sent back the messengers to their master forthwith, at the same time making preparations for war by entering into alliance with various Syrian kings, and particularly with the powerful king of Soba.[1] David took the initiative, and sent his army under command of Joab against Rabbath-Ammon. The Syrians advanced to the relief of the besieged city; but Joab divided his forces, and, leaving his brother Abishai to hold the Ammonites in the town in check, proceeded himself against the Syrians and repulsed them. On their afterwards threatening to renew the attack in increased force, David went against them in strength and defeated them at Helam "on the river." It seems that as a result of this the kingdom of Soba was broken up and that of Damascus was made tributary. Rabbath-Ammon could not now hold out any longer, and the Ammonites shared the fate of their Moabite brethren. Finally, Edom was about the same time coerced and depopulated; and thus was fulfilled the vision of Balaam,—the youngest of the four Hebrew nationalities trod the three elder under his feet.

So far as external foes were concerned, David henceforward had peace; but new dangers arose at home within his own family. At once by ill-judged leniency and equally ill-timed severity he had

---

[1] Soba appears to have been situated somewhat to the north of Damascus, and to have bordered on the west with Hamath. The Aramæans were beginning even at that period to press westwards; the Hittites, Phœnicians, and Israelites had common interests against them. To the kingdom of Soba succeeded afterwards that of Damascus,

completely alienated his son Absalom, who, after Amnon's death, was heir-apparent to the throne. Absalom organised a revolt against his father, and to foster it availed himself of a misunderstanding which had arisen between David and the men of Judah, probably because they thought they were not treated with sufficient favour. The revolt had its focus in Hebron; Ahithophel, a man of Judah, was its soul; Amasa, also of Judah, its arm; but the rest of Israel was also drawn into the rebellion, and only the territory to the east of Jordan remained faithful.

Thither David betook himself with precipitancy, for the outbreak had taken him completely by surprise. At Mahanaim, which had once before been the centre from which the kingdom was regained, he collected his faithful followers around him with his six hundred Cherethites and Pelethites for a nucleus, Absalom, against Ahithophel's advice, allowing him time for this. In the neighbourhood of Mahanaim, in the wood of Ephraim, the decisive blow was struck. Absalom fell, and with his death the rebellion was at an end. It was Joseph that, in the first instance, penitently sent a deputation to the king to bring him back. Judah, on the other hand, continued to hold aloof. Ultimately a piece of finesse on the king's part had the effect of bringing Judah also to its allegiance, though at the cost of kindling such jealousy between Israel and Judah that Sheba the Benjamite raised a new revolt, this time of Israelites, which was soon, however, repressed by Joab.

David seems to have died soon afterwards. His historical importance is very great. Judah and Jerusalem were wholly his creation, and, though the united kingdom of Israel founded by him and Saul together soon fell to pieces, the recollection of it nevertheless continued in all time to be proudly cherished by the whole body of the people. His personal character has been often treated with undue disparagement. For this we must chiefly blame his canonisation by the later Jewish tradition which made a Levitical saint of him and a pious hymn-writer.

It then becomes a strange inconsistency that he caused military prisoners to be treated with barbarity, and the bastard sons of Saul to be hanged up before the Lord in Gibeon. But if we take him as we find him, an antique king in a barbarous age, our judgment of him will be much more favourable. The most daring courage was combined in him with tender susceptibility; even after he had ascended the throne he continued to retain the charm of a pre-eminent and at the same time childlike personality. Even his conduct in the affair of Uriah is not by any means wholly to his discredit; not many kings can be mentioned who would have shown repentance public and deep such as he manifested at Nathan's rebuke. Least to his credit was his weakness in relation to his sons and to Joab. On the other hand, the testament attributed to him in 1 Kings ii. cannot be justly laid to his charge; it is the libel of a later hand seeking to invest him with a fictitious glory. In like manner it is unjust to hold him responsible for the deaths of Abner and Amasa, or to attribute to him any conspiracy with the hierocracy for the destruction of Saul, and thus to deprive him of the authorship of the elegy in 2 Sam. i., which certainly was not the work of a hypocrite.

Solomon had already reached the throne, some time before his father's death, not in virtue of hereditary right, but by palace intrigue which had the support of the bodyguard of the Six Hundred. His glory was not purchased on the battlefield. So far was he from showing military capacity that he allowed a new Syrian kingdom to arise at Damascus, a far more dangerous thing for Israel than that of Soba which had been destroyed, and which it succeeded. During this reign Edom also regained its independence, nothing but the port of Elath remaining in Solomon's hands. As regards Moab and Ammon, we have no information; it is not improbable that they also revolted. But if war was not Solomon's forte, he certainly took much greater pains than either of his predecessors in matters of internal administration; according to tradition, the wisdom of the ruler and the judge was his special "gift."

The absorption of the Canaanites, a process which acquired accelerated speed with the establishment of the kingdom, appears to have become tolerably complete in Solomon's time. As an element in the community their presence tended towards tribe-dissolution and state-consolidation, and in this respect also their assimilation was an important political result.

Solomon could now for the first time venture, without troubling himself about tribes and clans, to divide the kingdom into twelve geographical provinces, with a royal governor in charge of each. Judah alone he exempted from this arrangement, as if to show special favour. For his aim was less the advantage of his subjects than the benefit of his exchequer, and the same object appears in his horse traffic (1 Kings ix. 19), his Ophir trade (1 Kings x. 11), and his cession of territory to Hiram (1 Kings ix. 11). His passions were architecture, a gorgeous court, and the harem, in which he sought to rival other Oriental kings, as for example his Egyptian father-in-law. For this he required copious means, forced labour, tribute in kind and money. He had especially at heart the extension and improvement of Jerusalem as a strong and splendid capital; the temple which he built was only a portion of his vast citadel, which included within its precincts a

FOUNDATION OF THE KINGDOM.

number of private and public buildings designed for various uses.

It is plain that new currents were introduced into the stream of the nation's development by such a king as this. As formerly, after the occupation, Canaanite culture had come in, so now, after the establishment of the kingdom, the floodgate was open for the admission of Oriental civilisation in a deeper and wider sense. Whatever the personal motives which led to it may have been, the results were very important, and by no means disadvantageous on the whole. On the basis of the firmer administration now introduced, stability and order could rest; Judah had no cause to regret its acceptance of this yoke. Closer intercourse with foreign lands widened the intellectual horizon of the people, and at the same time awakened it to a deeper sense of its own peculiar individuality. If Solomon imported Phœnician and Egyptian elements into the worship of Jehovah at his court temple, the rigid old Israelite indeed might naturally enough take offence (Exod. xx. 24–26), but the temple itself nevertheless ultimately acquired a great and positive importance for religion. It need not be denied that mischievous consequences of various kinds slipped in along with the good. The king, however, can hardly be blamed for his conduct in erecting in the neighbourhood of Jerusalem altars to deities of Ammon and Egypt. For those altars remained undisturbed until the time of Josiah, although between Solomon and him there reigned more than one pious king who would certainly have destroyed them had he found them as offensive as did the author of Deuteronomy.

CHAPTER IV.

FROM JEROBOAM I. TO JEROBOAM II.

AFTER the death of Solomon the discontent which had been aroused by his innovations, and especially by the rigour of his government, openly showed itself against his successor; and when Rehoboam curtly refused the demands which had been laid before him by an assembly of the elders at Shechem, they withdrew from their allegiance and summoned to be their king the Ephraimite Jeroboam ben Nebat, who already had made an abortive attempt at revolt from Solomon, and afterwards had taken refuge in Egypt. Only Judah and Jerusalem remained faithful to the house of David. Among the causes of the revolt of the ten tribes, jealousy of Judah must certainly be reckoned as one. The power of Joseph had been weakened by the Philistines, and by the establishment of the monarchy the centre of gravity had been shifted from the north, where it naturally lay. But now it was restored to its old and real seat; for it was not situated in Judah, but in Joseph. Monarchy itself, however, was not abolished by the revolting tribes, conclusively showing how unavoidable and how advantageous that institution was now felt to be; but at the same time they did not refrain from attempts to combine its advantages with those of anarchy, a folly which was ultimately the cause of their ruin. As for their departure from the Mosaic cultus observed at Jerusalem, on the other hand, it was first alleged against them as a sin only by the later Jews. At the time religion put no obstacle in the way of their separation; on the contrary, it actually suggested and promoted it (Ahijah of Shiloh). The Jerusalem cultus had not yet come to be regarded as the alone legitimate; that instituted by Jeroboam at Bethel and at Dan was recognised as equally right; images of the Deity were exhibited in all three places, and indeed in every place where a house of God was found. So far as the religious and intellectual life of the nation was concerned, there was no substantial difference between the two kingdoms, except indeed in so far as new displays of vigorous initiative generally proceeded from Israel.[1]

Rehoboam did not readily accept the situation; he sought to reduce the revolt by force of arms.

[1] Even in the Deuteronomic redaction of the Book of Kings, it is true, and still more by the Chronicler, the political rebellion of Israel is regarded as having been ecclesiastical and religious in its character. The Book of Chronicles regards Samaria as a heathen kingdom, and recognises Judah alone as Israel. But in point of fact Judah takes up the history of Israel only after the fall of Samaria; see chapters vi., vii.

With what degree of success is shown by the fact that his rival found himself constrained to take up his residence at Peniel (near Mahanaim) on the other side of Jordan. The invasion of Shishak, however, who took Jerusalem and burnt it, seems to have given Jeroboam a breathing space. The feud continued indeed, but Rehoboam could no longer dream of bringing back the ten tribes. The scale by-and-by turned in Israel's favour. King Baasha, who had seated himself on the throne in place of Nadab, Jeroboam's son, took the offensive, and Asa ben Rehoboam had no help for it but to call in Benhadad of Damascus against his adversary. In this way he gained his immediate purpose, it is true, but by the most dangerous of expedients.

Baasha's son Elah was supplanted by his vizier Zimri, who, however, was in his turn unable to hold his own against Omri, who had supreme command of the army. Against Omri there arose in another part of the country a rival, Tibni ben Ginath, who succeeded in maintaining some footing until his death, when Omri became supreme. Omri must be regarded as the founder of the first dynasty, in the proper sense of that word, in Israel, and as the second founder of the kingdom itself, to which he gave a permanent capital in Samaria. The Bible has hardly anything to tell us about him, but his importance is evident from the fact that among the

Assyrians "the kingdom of Omri"[1] was the ordinary name of Israel. According to the inscription of Mesha, it was he who again subjugated Moab, which had become independent at the death of David or of Solomon. He was not so successful against the Damascenes, to whom he had to concede certain privileges in his own capital (1 Kings xx. 34).[2]

Ahab, who succeeded Omri his father, seems during the greater part of his reign to have in some sort acknowledged Syrian suzerainty. In no other way can we account for the fact that in the battle of Karkar against the Assyrians (854 B.C.) a contingent was contributed by him. But this very battle made the political situation so clear to him that he was led to break off his relations with Damascus. With this began a series of ferocious attacks on Israel by Benhadad and Hazael. They were met by Ahab with courage and success, but in the third year of that fifty years' war he fell in the battle at Ramoth-Gilead (c. 851).

(*After* the events recorded in 1 Kings xx., a forced alliance with Damascus on the part of Samaria is incredible; but the idea of spontaneous friendly rela-

[1] Bit Humri, like οἶκος Αυσανίου, and similar territorial names in Syriac.

[2] Omri's accession is to be placed somewhere about 900 B.C. It is a date, and the first, that can be determined with some precision, if we place the battle of Karkar (854) near the end of Ahab's reign, and take the servitude of Moab, which lasted forty years and ended with Ahab's death, to begin in Omri's first decade.

tions is also inadmissible. Schrader indeed finds support for the latter theory in 1 Kings xx. 34; but in that passage there is no word of any offensive or defensive alliance between the rival kings; all that is stated is that Ahab releases the captive Benhadad on condition (בברית) that the latter undertakes certain obligations, particularly those of keeping the peace and restoring the cities which had been taken. By this arrangement no change was made in the previously strained relations of the two kingdoms; and, moreover, the ברית was not kept (xxii. 1 *seq.*). Not much nearer the truth than the preceding is the view that the danger threatened by Assyria drove the kings of Syria and Palestine into one another's arms, and so occasioned an alliance beween Ahab and Benhadad. For if feelings of hostility existed at all between the two last-named, then Ahab could not do otherwise than congratulate himself that in the person of Shalmaneser II. there had arisen against Benhadad an enemy who would be able to keep him effectually in check. That Shalmaneser might prove dangerous to himself probably did not at that time occur to him; but if it had he would still have chosen the remote in preference to the immediately threatening evil. For it was the political existence of Israel that was at stake in the struggle with Damascus; in such circumstances every ally would of course be welcome, every enemy of the enemy would be hailed as a friend, and the political wisdom which Max Duncker attributes to Ahab would have been nothing less than unpardonable folly. The state of matters was at the outset in this respect just what it continued to be throughout the subsequent course of events; the Assyrian danger grew in subsequent years, and with it grew the hostility between Damascus and Samaria. This fact admits only of one explanation—that the Israelites utilised to the utmost of their power for their own protection against the Syrians the difficulties into which the latter were thrown by Shalmaneser II., and that these in their turn, when the Assyians gave them respite, were all the fiercer in their revenge. On the evidence of the monuments and the Bible we may even venture to assert that it was the Assyrian attacks upon Damascus which at that time preserved Israel from becoming Aramaic,—of course only because Israel made the most of them for her political advantage.

Assuming that Ahab the Israelite (Ahabu Sirlaai) fought in the battle of Karkar (854) on the side of the king of Damascus, it was only because he could not help himself; but if it is actually the case that he did so, the battle of Karkar must have taken place *before* the events recorded in I Kings xx.)

The Moabites took advantage of an accession under such critical circumstances to shake off the yoke imposed by Omri forty years before; an accurate account of their success, obviously written while the impression of it was still fresh,[1] has come down to us in the famous inscription of King Mesha. Ahaziah, Ahab's immediate successor, was obliged to accept the situation; after his early death a futile attempt again to subjugate them was made by his brother Joram. Such a campaign was possible to him only in the event of the Syrians keeping quiet, and in point of fact it would appear that they were not in a position to follow up the advantage they had gained at Ramoth; doubtless they were hampered by the inroads of the Assyrians in 850 and 849. As soon as they got a little respite, however, they lost no time in attacking Joram, driving him into his capital, where they besieged him. Samaria had already been brought to the utmost extremities of famine, when suddenly the enemy raised the siege on account of a report of an invasion of their own land by the "Egyptians and Hittites." Possibly we ought to understand by these the Assyrians rather, who in 846 renewed their attacks upon Syria; to ordinary people in Israel the Assyrians were an unknown quantity, for which it would be natural in popular story to substitute something more familiar. This turn of affairs relieved Joram from his straits; it would even seem that, favoured by a change of dynasty at Damascus, he had succeeded in taking from the Syrians the fortress of

---

[1] It is obvious that Mesha's narrative is to be taken with 2 Kings i. 1, and not with 2 Kings iii.

Ramoth in Gilead, which had been the object of Ahab's unsuccessful endeavours, when suddenly there burst upon the house of Omri the overwhelming catastrophe for which the prophets had long been preparing.

When the prophets first made their appearance, some time before the beginning of the Philistine war, they were a novel phenomenon in Israel; but in the interval they had become so naturalised that they now had a recognised and essential place in connection with the religion of Jehovah. They had in the process divested themselves of much that had originally characterised them, but they still retained their habit of appearing in companies and living together in societies, and also that of wearing a peculiar distinctive dress. These societies of theirs had no ulterior aims; the rabbinical notion that they were schools and academies in which the study of the Torah and of sacred history was pursued imports later ideas into an earlier time. First-rate importance on the whole cannot be claimed for the Nebiim, but occasionally there arose amongst them a man in whom the spirit which was cultivated within their circles may be said to have risen to the explosive pitch. Historical influence was exercised at no time save by these individuals, who rose above their order and even placed themselves in opposition to it, but always at the same time had their base of operations within it. The prototype of this class of exceptional prophets, whom we not unjustly have been accustomed to regard as the true, is Elijah of Thisbe, the contemporary of Ahab.

In compliment to Jezebel his wife, Ahab had set up in Samaria a temple with richly endowed religious services in honour of the Tyrian Baal. In doing so he had no intention of renouncing Jehovah; Jehovah continued to be the national God after whom he named his sons Ahaziah and Jehoram. The destruction of Jehovah's altars or the persecution of His prophets was not at all proposed, or even the introduction of a foreign cultus elsewhere than in Samaria. Jehovah's sovereignty over Israel being thus only remotely if at all imperilled, the popular faith found nothing specially offensive in a course of action which had been followed a hundred years before by Solomon also. Elijah alone was strenuous in his opposition; the masses did not understand him, and were far from taking his side. To him only, but not to the nation, did it seem like a halting between two opinions, an irreconcilable inconsistency, that Jehovah should be worshipped as Israel's God, and a chapel to Baal should at the same time be erected in Israel.

In solitary grandeur did this prophet tower conspicuously over his time; legend, and not history, could alone preserve the memory of his figure. There remains a vague impression that with him the development of Israel's conception of Jehovah entered upon a new stadium, rather than any data from which it can be ascertained wherein the contrast of the new with the old lay. After Jehovah, acting more immediately within the political sphere, had established the nation and kingdom, he now began in the spiritual sphere to operate against the foreign elements, the infusion of which previously had been permitted to go on almost unchecked.[1] The Rechabites, who arose at that time, protested in their zeal for Jehovah altogether against all civilisation which presupposes agriculture, and in their fundamental principles aimed at a recurrence to the primitive nomadic life of Israel in the wilderness; the Nazarites abstained at least from wine, the chief symbol of Dionysiac civilisation. In this, indeed, Elijah was not with them; had he been so, he would doubtless have been intelligible to the masses. But, comprehending as he did the spirit from which these demonstrations proceeded, he thought of Jehovah as a great principle which cannot coexist in the same heart with Baal. To him first was it revealed that we have not in the various departments of nature a variety of forces worthy of our worship, but that there exists over all but one Holy One and one Mighty One, who reveals Himself not in nature

[1] It is worth noticing how much more frequent from this period onwards proper names compounded with the word Jehovah become. Among the names of the judges and of the kings before Ahab in Israel and Asa in Judah, not a single instance occurs; thenceforward they become the rule.

but in law and righteousness in the world of man. The indignation he displayed against the judicial murder at Jezreel was as genuine and strong as that which he manifested against the worship of Baal in Samaria; the one was as much a crime against Jehovah as the other.

Elijah ascended to heaven before he had actually achieved much in the world. The idea which his successors took from him was that it was necessary to make a thorough clearance from Samaria of the Baal worship and of the house of Ahab as well. For this practical end Elisha made use of practical means. When Elijah, after the murder of Naboth, had suddenly appeared before Ahab and threatened him with a violent end, an officer of high command had been present, Jehu ben Nimshi, and he had never forgotten the incident. He now found himself at the head of the troops at Ramoth-Gilead after the withdrawal to Jezreel of Joram ben Ahab from the field to be healed of his wound. To Elisha the moment seemed a suitable one for giving to Jehu, in Jehovah's name, the command now to carry out Elijah's threat against the house of Ahab. Jehu gained over the captains of the army, and carried out so well the task with which the prophet had commissioned him that not a single survivor of Ahab's dynasty or of his court was left. He next extirpated Baal and his worshippers in Samaria. From that date no worship of foreign gods seems ever to have recurred in Israel. Idolatry indeed continued to subsist, but the images, stones, and trees, even the teraphim apparently, belonged to the cultus of Jehovah, or were at least brought into relation with it.

Jehu founded the second and last dynasty of the kingdom of Samaria. His inheritance from the house of Omri included the task of defending himself against the Syrians. The forces at his disposal being insufficient for this, he resorted to the expedient of seeking to urge the Assyrians to renew their hostilities against the Aramæans. For this end his ambassadors carried presents to Shalmaneser II.; these were not of a regular but only of an occasional character, but the vanity of the great king represents them as the tribute of a vassal. In the years 842 and 839 Assyrian campaigns against Hazael of Damascus actually took place; then they were intermitted for a long time, and the kings of Samaria, Jehu, and his two successors were left to their own resources. These were evil times for Israel. With a barbarity never relaxed the frontier war went on in Gilead, where Ammon and Moab showed themselves friendly to the Syrian cause (Amos i.); occasionally great expeditions took place, one of which brought King Hazael to the very walls of Jerusalem. It was only with the greatest difficulty that Israel's independence was maintained. Once more religion went hand in hand with the national cause; the prophet Elisha was the mainstay of the kings in the struggle with the Syrians, "the chariot and horsemen of Israel." Joash ben Joahaz ben Jehu at last succeeded in inflicting upon Syria several blows which proved decisive. Thenceforward Israel had nothing to fear from that quarter. Under Joash's son, Jeroboam II., the kingdom even reached a height of external power which recalled the times of David. Moab was again subdued; southwards the frontier extended to the brook of the Arabah (Amos vi. 14), and northward to Hamath.

CHAPTER V.

THE LIFE OF MEN IN OLD ISRAEL.

BEFORE proceeding to consider the rise of those prophets who were the makers of the new Israel, it will not be out of place here to cast a glance backwards upon the old order of things which perished with the kingdom of Samaria. With reference to any period earlier than the century 850–750 B.C., we can hardly be said to possess any statistics. For, while the facts of history admit of being handed down with tolerable accuracy through a considerable time, a contemporary literature is indispensable for the description of standing conditions. But it was within this period that Hebrew literature first flourished—after the Syrians had been finally repulsed, it would seem. Writing of course had been practised from a much earlier period, but only in formal instruments, mainly upon stone. At an early period also the historical sense of the people developed itself in connection with their religion; but it found its expression in songs, which in the first instance were handed down by word of mouth only. Literature began with the collection and writing out of those songs; the "Book of the Wars of the Lord" and the "Book of Jashar" were the oldest historical books. The transition was next made to the writing of prose history with the aid of legal documents and family reminiscences; a large portion of this early historiography has been preserved to us in the Books of Judges, Samuel, and Kings. Contemporaneously also certain collections of laws and decisions of the priests, of which we have an example in Ex. xxi., xxii., were committed to writing. Somewhat later, perhaps, the legends about the patriarchs and primitive times, the origin of which cannot be assigned to a very early date,[1] received literary shape. Specially remarkable is the rise of a written prophecy. The question why it was that Elijah and Elisha committed nothing to writing, while Amos a hundred years later is an author, hardly admits of any other answer than that in the interval a non-literary had developed into a literary age. How rapid the process was may be gathered from a comparison between the singularly broken utter-

[1] Even the Jehovistic narratives about the patriarchs belong to the time when Israel had already become a powerful kingdom; Moab, Ammon, and Edom had been subjugated (Gen. xxvii. 29), and vigorous frontier wars were being carried on with the Syrians about Gilead (Gen. xxxi. 52). In Gen. xxvii. 40 allusion is made to the constantly repeated subjugations of Edom by Judah, alternating with successful revolts on the part of the former; see Delitzsch on באשׁר.

ances of the earlier oracle contained in Isa. xv., xvi. with the orations of Isaiah himself.

We begin our survey with that of the family relations. Polygamy was rare, monogamy the rule; but the right of concubinage was unlimited. While a high position was accorded both by affection and custom to the married wife, traces still existed of a state of society in which she was regarded as property that went with the inheritance. The marriage of relations was by no means prohibited; no offence was taken at the circumstance that Abraham was the husband of his sister (by a different mother). Parents had full power over their children; they had the right to sell and even to sacrifice them. In this respect, however, the prevailing usage was mild, as also in regard to slaves, who socially held a position of comparative equality with their masters, and even enjoyed some measure of legal protection. Slavery, it is plain, had not the same political importance as with the Greeks and Romans; it could have been abolished without any shock to the foundations of the state.

Throughout this period agriculture and gardening continued to be regarded as man's normal calling (Gen. iii. 4); the laws contained in Exod. xxi.–xxiii. rest entirely upon this assumption. To dwell in peace under his vine and under his fig-tree was the ideal of every genuine Israelite. Only

LIFE UNDER THE OLD KINGDOM. 73

in a few isolated districts, as in the country to the east of Jordan and in portions of Judah, did the pastoral life predominate. Art and industry were undeveloped, and were confined to the production of simple domestic necessaries.

Commerce was in old time followed exclusively by the Canaanite towns, so that the word "Canaanite" was used in the general sense of "trader." But by-and-by Israel began to tread in Canaan's footsteps (Hos. xii. 8, 9 [A.V. 7, 8]).[1] The towns grew more influential than the country; money notably increased; and the zeal of piety was quite unable to arrest the progress of the change which set in. The kings themselves, from Solomon onwards, were the first to set the bad example; they eagerly sought to acquire suitable harbours, and in company or in competition with the Tyrians entered upon large commercial transactions. The extortions of the corn-market, the formation of large estates, the frequency of mortgages, all show that the small peasant proprietorship was unable to hold its own against the accumulations of wealth. The wage-receiving class increased, and cases in which free Hebrews sold themselves into slavery were not rare.

On all hands the material progress of the com-

[1] "Canaan (*i.e.*, Ephraim Canaanised) has deceitful balances in his hand, and loves to overreach. Ephraim indeed saith, I am become rich, I have gained wealth; but all his profits will not suffice for (expiation of) the guilt which he has incurred."

monwealth made itself felt, the old simplicity of manners disappeared, and luxury increased. Buildings of hewn stone began to be used even by private individuals. The towns, especially the chief ones, were fortified; and in time of war refuge was sought in them, and not as formerly in woods and caves. Even in the time of David the Israelites always fought on foot; but now horses and chariots were regarded as indispensable. The bow came to be the principal weapon of offence, and a military class appears to have sprung up.

The monarchy retained in the kingdom of the ten tribes its military character; the commander-in-chief was the first person in the state after the king. In internal affairs its interference was slight; with systematic despotism it had little in common, although of course within its narrow sphere it united executive and legislative functions. It was little more than the greatest house in Israel. The highest official was called "master of the household." The court ultimately grew into a capital, the municipal offices of which were held by royal officials. The provinces had governors who, however, in time of war withdrew to the capital (1 Kings xx.); the presumption is that their sole charge was collection of the revenue.

The state was not charged with affairs of internal administration; all parties were left free to maintain their own interests. Only in cases in which conflicts had emerged in consequence was the king approached. Ruling and judging were regarded as one and the same; there was but one word for both (2 Kings xv. 5). Still, the king was not altogether the only judge; there were, in fact, a number of independent jurisdictions. Wherever within a particular circle the power lay, there the right of judging was also found, whether exercised by heads of families and communities or by warriors and powerful lords. It was only because the king was the most powerful that he was regarded as the judge of last resort; but it was equally permitted to apply to him from the first. Of method and rule in these things there was but little; a man was glad to find any court to receive his complaint. Of course without complaint one got no justice. The administration of justice was at best but a scanty supplement to the practice of self-help. The heir of the murdered man would not forego the right of blood revenge; but his family or the commune gave him aid, and in case of need took his place, for bloodshed had at all hazards to be atoned for.

The firm establishment of civil order was rendered all the more difficult by the continual wars and violent changes of dynasty which ever and anon made its very existence problematical. Power, which is more important than righteousness to a judicatory, was what the government was wanting in. In the simpler social conditions of the earlier time a state which was adapted merely for purposes of war might easily be found to work satisfactorily enough, but a more complex order of things had now arisen. Social problems had begun to crop up; for the poor and the proletariat the protection of a thoughtful government had come to be required, but was not forthcoming.

But these defects did not check all progress. The weakness of the government, the want of political consolidation, were insufficient to arrest intellectual advance or to corrupt the prevailing moral tone and feeling for justice; in fact it was precisely in this period (the period in which the main part of the Jehovistic history must have been written) that the intellectual and moral culture of the people stood at its highest. Even when the machinery of the monarchy had got out of order, the organisation of the families and communes continued to subsist; the smaller circles of social life remained comparatively untouched by the catastrophes that shook the greater. Above all, the national religion supplied the spiritual life with an immovable basis.

The favourite illustrations of the power of religion in the Israel of that period are drawn from the instances of great prophets who raised kings out of the dust and smote them to it again. But the influence and importance of these is generally exaggerated in the accounts we have. That among them there occasionally occurred manifestations of such power as to give a new turn in history is indeed true; a figure like that of Elijah is no mere invention. But such a man as he was a prophecy of the future rather than an actual agent in shaping the present. On the whole, religion was a peaceful influence, conserving rather than assailing the existing order of things. The majority of the prophets were no revolutionists; rather in fact were they always too much inclined to prophesy in accordance with the wishes of the party in power. Besides, in ordinary circumstances their influence was inferior to that of the priests, who were servants of royalty at the chief sanctuaries, and everywhere attached to the established order.

The Torah of Jehovah still continued to be their special charge. It was not even now a code or law in our sense of the word; Jehovah had not yet made His Testament; He was still living and active in Israel. But the Torah appears during this period to have withdrawn itself somewhat from the business of merely pronouncing legal decisions and to have begun to move in a freer field. It now consisted in teaching the knowledge of God, in showing the right God-given way where men were not sure of themselves. Many of the counsels of the priests had become a common stock of moral convictions, which, indeed, were all of them referred to Jehovah as their author, yet had ceased to be matters of direct revelation. Nevertheless the Torah had still occupation enough, the progressive life of the nation ever affording matter for new questions.

Although in truth the Torah and the moral influence of Jehovah upon the national life were things much weightier and much more genuinely Israelitic than the cultus, yet this latter held on the whole a higher place in public opinion. To the ordinary man it was not moral but liturgical acts that seemed to be truly religious. Altars of Jehovah occurred everywhere, with sacred stones and trees—the latter either artificial (Asheras) or natural—beside them; it was considered desirable also to have water in the neighbourhood (brazen sea). In cases where a temple stood before the altar it contained an ephod and teraphim, a kind of images before which the lot was cast by the priest. Of the old simplicity the cultus retained nothing; at the great sanctuaries especially (Bethel, Gilgal, Beersheba) it had become very elaborate. Its chief seasons were the agricultural festivals—the passover, the feast of weeks, and most especially the feast of the ingathering at the close of the year. These were the only occasions of public worship properly so called, at which every one was expected to attend; in other cases each worshipper sought the presence of God only in special circumstances, as for example at the beginning and at the end of particular undertakings. The cultus, as to place, time, matter, and form, belonged almost entirely to the inheritance which Israel had received from Canaan; to distinguish what belonged to the worship of Jehovah from that which belonged to Baal was no easy matter.[1] It was the channel through which also paganism could and did ever anew gain admittance into the worship of Jehovah. Yet that publicity of the cultus which arose out of the very nature of Jehovah cannot but have acted as a corrective against the most fatal excesses.

As for the substance of the national faith, it was summed up principally in the proposition that Jehovah is the God of Israel. "God" was equivalent to "helper;" that was the meaning of the word. "Help," assistance in all occasions of life, —that was what Israel looked for from Jehovah, not "salvation" in the theological sense. The forgiveness of sins was a matter of subordinate importance; it was involved in the "help," and was a matter not of faith but of experience. The relation between the people and God was a natural one as that of son to father; it did not rest upon observance of the conditions of a pact. But it was not on that account always equally lively and hearty; Jehovah was regarded as having varieties of mood. To secure and retain His favour sacrifices were

---

[1] The description of the cultus by the Prophet Hosea shows this very clearly. It is obvious enough, however, that the object was to serve *Jehovah*, and not any foreign deity, by this worship.

useful; by them prayer and thanksgiving were seconded.

Another main article of faith was that Jehovah judges and recompenses, not after death (then all men were thought to be alike), but upon the earth. Here, however, but little account was taken of the individual; over him the wheel of destiny remorselessly rolled; his part was resignation and not hope. Not in the career of the individual but in the fate of families and nations did the righteousness of Jehovah find scope for its manifestation; and this is the only reason why the religion could dispense with the conceptions of heaven and hell. For the rest, it was not always easy to bring the second article into correlation with the first; in practice the latter received the superior place.

It need hardly be said that superstition of every kind also abounded. But the superstition of the Israelites had as little real religious significance as had that poetical view of nature which the Hebrews doubtless shared in greater or less degree with all the other nations of antiquity.

CHAPTER VI.

THE FALL OF SAMARIA.

UNDER King Jeroboam II., two years before a great earthquake that served ever after for a date to all who had experienced it, there occurred at Bethel, the greatest and most conspicuous sanctuary of Jehovah in Israel, a scene full of significance. The multitude were assembled there with gifts and offerings for the observance of a festival, when there stepped forward a man whose grim seriousness interrupted the joy of the feast. It was a Judæan, Amos of Tekoa, a shepherd from the wilderness bordering on the Dead Sea. Into the midst of the joyful tones of the songs which with harp and tabor were being sung at the sacred banquet he brought the discordant note of the mourner's wail. For over all the joyous stir of busy life his ear caught the sounds of death: "The virgin of Israel is fallen, never more to rise; lies prostrate in her own land with no one to lift her up." He prophesied as close at hand the downfall of the kingdom which just at that moment was rejoicing most in the consciousness of power, and the deportation of the people to a far-off northern land.

There was something rotten in the state of Israel in spite of the halcyon days it enjoyed under Jeroboam II. From the indirect results of war, from changes in the tenure and in the culture of the soil, from defective administration of justice, the humbler classes had much to suffer; they found that the times were evil. But it was not this that caused Amos to foresee the end of Israel, not a mere vague foreboding of evil that forced him to leave his flocks; the dark cloud that threatened on the horizon was plain enough—the Assyrians. Once already at an earlier date they had directed their course south-westwards, without, however, on that occasion becoming a source of danger to the Israelites. But now that the bulwark against the Assyrians, Aram of Damascus, was falling into ruins, a movement of these against Lebanon in the time of Jeroboam II. opened to Israel the alarming prospect that sooner or later they would have to meet the full force of the irresistible avalanche.

What then? The common man was in no position truly to estimate the danger; and, so far as he apprehended it, he lived in the firm faith that Jehovah would not abandon His people in their straits. The governing classes prided themselves on the military resources of Israel, or otherwise tried to dismiss from their minds all thought

THE FALL OF SAMARIA.

of the gravity of the situation. But Amos heard the question distinctly enough, and did not hesitate to answer it: the downfall of Israel is imminent. It was nothing short of blasphemy to utter anything of this kind, for everything, Jehovah Himself included, depended on the existence of the nation. But the most astounding thing has yet to come; not Asshur, but Jehovah Himself, is bringing about the overthrow of Israel; through Asshur it is Jehovah that is triumphing over Israel. A paradoxical thought—as if the national God were to cut the ground from under His own feet! For the faith in Jehovah as the God of Israel was a faith that He intervenes on behalf of His people against all enemies, against the whole world; precisely in times of danger was religion shown by staying oneself upon this faith. Jehovah might indeed, of course, hide His face for a time, but not definitely; in the end He ever arose at last against all opposing powers. "The day of the Lord" was an object of hope in all times of difficulty and oppression; it was understood as self-evident that the crisis would certainly end in favour of Israel. Amos took up the popular conception of that day; but how thoroughly did he change its meaning! "Woe to them who long for the day of the Lord!—What to you is the day of the Lord? It is darkness, not light." His own opposition to the popular conception is formulated in a paradox which he prefixes as theme to the principal section of his book:—"Us alone does Jehovah know," say the Israelites, drawing from this the inference that He is on their side, and of course must take their part. "You only do I know," Amos represents Jehovah as saying, "therefore do I visit upon you all your sins."

If the question, Whereon did Jehovah's relation to Israel ultimately rest? be asked, the answer, according to the popular faith, must substantially be that it rested on the fact that Jehovah was worshipped in Israel and not among the heathen, that in Israel were His altars and His dwelling. His cultus was the bond between Him and the nation; when therefore it was desired to draw the bond still closer, the solemn services of religion were redoubled. But to the conception of Amos Jehovah is no judge capable of accepting a bribe; with the utmost indignation he repudiates the notion that it is possible to influence Him by gifts and offerings. Though Israel alone has served Him he does not on that account apply any other standard to it than to other nations (chaps. i., ii.). If Israel is better known to Him, it does not follow that on that account He shuts His eyes and blindly takes a side. Neither Jehovah nor His prophet recognises two moral standards; right is everywhere right, wrong always wrong, even though committed against Israel's worst enemies (ii. 1). What Jehovah demands is righteousness,—nothing more and nothing less;

what He hates is injustice. Sin or offence to the Deity is a thing of purely moral character; with such emphasis this doctrine had never before been heard. Morality is that for the sake of which all other things exist; it is the alone essential thing in the world. It is no postulate, no idea, but at once a necessity and a fact, the most intensely living of personal powers—Jehovah the God of Hosts. In wrath, in ruin, this holy reality makes its existence known; it annihilates all that is hollow and false.

Amos calls Jehovah the God of Hosts, never the God of Israel. The nation as such is no religious conception to him; from its mere existence he cannot formulate any article of faith. Sometimes it seems as if he were denying Israel's prerogative altogether. He does not really do so, but at least the prerogative is conditional and involves a heavy responsibility. The saying in iii. 2 recalls Luke xii. 47. The proposition "Jehovah knows Israel" is in the mouth of Amos almost the same thing as "Israel knows Jehovah;" save only that this is not to be regarded as any merit on Israel's part, but as a manifestation of the grace of Jehovah, who has led His people by great deeds and holy men, and so made Himself known. Amos knows no other truth than that practical one which he has found among his own people and nowhere else, lying at the foundation of life and morality, and which he regards as the product of a divine providential ordering of history. From this point of view, so thoroughly Israelitish, he pronounces Israel's condemnation. He starts from premises generally conceded, but he accentuates them differently and draws from them divergent conclusions.

Amos was the founder, and the purest type, of a new phase of prophecy. The impending conflict of Asshur with Jehovah and Israel, the ultimate downfall of Israel, is its theme. Until that date there had subsisted in Palestine and Syria a number of petty kingdoms and nationalities, which had their friendships and enmities with one another, but paid no heed to anything outside their own immediate environment, and revolved, each on its own axis, careless of the outside world, until suddenly the Assyrians burst in upon them. These commenced the work which was carried on by the Babylonians, Persians, and Greeks, and completed by the Romans. They introduced a new factor, the conception of the world,—the world of course in the historical sense of that expression. In presence of that conception the petty nationalities lost their centre of gravity, brute fact dispelled their illusions, they flung their gods to the moles and to the bats (Isa. ii.). The prophets of Israel alone did not allow themselves to be taken by surprise by what had occurred, or to be plunged in despair; they solved by anticipation the

grim problem which history set before them. They
absorbed into their religion that conception of the
world which was destroying the religions of the
nations, even before it had been fully grasped by
the secular consciousness. Where others saw only
the ruin of everything that is holiest, they saw the
triumph of Jehovah over delusion and error. Whatever
else might be overthrown, the really worthy
remained unshaken. They recognised ideal powers
only, right and wrong, truth and falsehood; second
causes were matters of indifference to them, they
were no practical politicians. But they watched the
course of events attentively, nay, with passionate
interest. The present, which was passing before
them, became to them as it were the plot of a divine
drama which they watched with an intelligence that
anticipated the *dénouement*. Everywhere the same
goal of the development, everywhere the same laws.
The nations are the *dramatis personæ*, Israel the
hero, Jehovah the poet of the tragedy.

The canonical prophets, the series of whom begins
with Amos, were separated by an essential distinction
from the class which had preceded them and
which still continued to be the type of the common
prophet. They did not seek to kindle either the
enthusiasm or the fanaticism of the multitude; they
swam not with but against the stream. They were
not patriotic, at least in the ordinary acceptation of
that word; they prophesied not good but evil for

their people (Jer. xxviii. 8). Until their time the nation had sprung up out of the conception of Jehovah; now the conception of Jehovah was casting the nation into the shade. The natural bond between the two was severed, and the relation was henceforward viewed as conditional. As God of the righteousness which is the law of the whole universe, Jehovah could be Israel's God only in so far as in Israel the right was recognised and followed. The ethical element destroyed the national character of the old religion. It still addressed itself, to be sure, more to the nation and to society at large than to the individual; it insisted less upon a pure heart than upon righteous institutions; but nevertheless the first step towards universalism had been accomplished, towards at once the general diffusion and the individualisation of religion. Thus, although the prophets were far from originating a new conception of God, they none the less were the founders of what has been called "ethical monotheism." But with them this ethical monotheism was no product of the "self-evolution of dogma," but a progressive step which had been called forth simply by the course of events. The providence of God brought it about that this call came at an opportune period, and not too suddenly. The downfall of the nation did not take place until the truths and precepts of religion were already strong enough to be able to live on alone; to the prophets belongs the merit of having recognised the independence of these, and of having secured perpetuity to Israel by refusing to allow the conception of Jehovah to be involved in the ruin of the kingdom. They saved faith by destroying illusion.

The event which Amos had foreseen was not long in coming. The Israelites flew spontaneously, like "silly doves," into the net of the Assyrians. Zechariah ben Jeroboam was overthrown after a short reign, Shallum his murderer and successor was also unable to hold his own, and was followed after the horrors of a civil war by Menahem ben Gadi (745 B.C.). But Menahem, in the presence of domestic (and perhaps also foreign) assailants,[1] had no other resort than to purchase by payment of a great tribute the assistance of King Tiglath-pileser II., who at that time was giving new force to the Assyrian predominance

[1] It is not inconceivable that the wars carried on by Tiglath-pileser II. against Hamath had some connection with his interventions in favour of Menahem. The kingdom of Hamath, which may have been threatened by Jeroboam II., may have availed itself of the state of matters which followed his death to secure its own aggrandisement at Israel's expense; in correspondence with this attack from the northern side another by Judah in concert with Hamath may well have been made from the south. In this way, though not without the aid of pure hypothesis, it might be possible to fit into the general historical connection the fragmentary Assyrian notices about Azariah of Judah and his relations to Hamath. But in that case it would certainly be necessary to assume that the Assyrians were badly informed as to the nature of the relations between Hamath and Judah, and also as to the individual who at that time held the throne of Judah. Uzziah (= Azariah), who in his old age had become a leper, could only nominally at best have been king of Judah then.

in these regions. By such means he succeeded in attaining his immediate end, but the further consequence was that the rival party in the state turned for support to Egypt, and Palestine now became the arena of conflict between the two great world-powers.

Menahem transmitted his kingdom to Pekahiah; Pekahiah was murdered about 735 B.C. by Pekah, and Pekah himself shortly afterwards was overthrown. All this happened within a few years. It would have been possible to conjecture the state of the country in these circumstances, even if we had not been informed of it by means of the prophetical book of Hosea, which dates from the time when the Assyrians had begun indeed to tamper with the country, but had not yet shown their full design. After the death of Jeroboam II. there had been wild outbursts of partisan war; none of the kings who in quick succession appeared and disappeared had real power, none established order. It was as if the danger from without, which was only too obviously threatening the existence of the kingdom, had already dissolved all internal bonds; every one was at war with his neighbour. Assyrians and Egyptians were called in to support this or that government; by such expedients the external confusion was, naturally, only increased. Was there any other quarter in which help could yet be sought? The people, led by the priests, turned to

THE FALL OF SAMARIA.

the altars of Jehovah, and outdid itself in pious works, as if by any such illusory means, out of all relation to the practical problem in hand, the gangrene of anarchy could possibly be healed. Still more zealous than Amos against the cultus was Hosea, not merely on the ground that it had the absurd motive of forcing Jehovah's favour, but also because it was of heathenish character, nature-worship and idolatry. That Jehovah is the true and only helper is certainly not denied by Hosea. But His help is coupled with the condition that Israel shall undergo a complete change, and of such a change he sees no prospect. On this account the downfall of the state is in Hosea's view inevitable, but not final ruin, only such an overthrow as is necessary for the transition to a new and fair recommencement. In Hosea's prophecies the relation between Jehovah and Israel is conceived of as dissoluble, and as actually on the point of being dissolved, but it has struck its roots so deep that it must inevitably at last establish itself again.

The first actual collision between Israel and Assyria occurred in 734. Resin, king of Damascus, and Pekah, king of Samaria, had united in an expedition against Judah, where at that time Ahaz ben Jotham occupied the throne. But Ahaz parried the blow by placing himself under the protection of the Assyrians, who perhaps would in any case have struck in against the alliance between

Aram and Israel. Tiglath-pileser made his first appearance in 734, first on the sea-coast of Palestine, and subsequently either in this or in the following year took up his quarters in the kingdom of the ten tribes. After he had ravaged Galilee and Gilead, he finally concluded a peace with Samaria conditionally on his receiving the head of King Pekah and a considerable yearly tribute. Hosea ben Elah was raised to the throne in Pekah's place and acknowledged by the Assyrian as a vassal. For some ten years he held his position quietly, regularly paying his dues. But when at the death of Tiglath-pileser the Syro-Palestinian kingdoms rebelled *en masse*, Samaria also was seized with the delirium of patriotic fanaticism (Isa. xxviii.). Relying upon the help of Seve, king of Ethiopia and Egypt, Hosea ventured on a revolt from Assyria. But the Egyptians left him in the lurch as soon as Shalmaneser IV., Tiglath-pileser's successor, invaded his territory. Before his capital had fallen, Hosea himself fell into the hands of the Assyrians. Samaria offered a desperate resistance, and succumbed only to Sargon, Shalmaneser's successor (721). Energetic measures were adopted by the victor for the pacification of the country; he carried all the inhabitants of mark into captivity to Calachene, Gozanitis, and Armenia. Much light is thrown upon the conditions of the national religion then and upon its subsequent development by the single fact that the exiled Israelites were absorbed by the surrounding heathenism without leaving a trace behind them, while the population of Judah, who had the benefit of a hundred years' respite, held their faith fast throughout the period of the Babylonian exile, and by means of it were able to maintain their own individuality afterwards in all the circumstances that arose. The fact that the fall of Samaria did not hinder but helped the religion of Jehovah is entirely due to the prophets. That they had foreseen the downfall of the state, and declared in the name of religion that it was inevitable, was a matter of much greater historical importance than the actual downfall itself.

CHAPTER VII.

THE DELIVERANCE OF JUDAH.

HITHERTO the small kingdom of Judah had stood in the background. Its political history had been determined almost exclusively by its relation to Israel. Under the dynasty of Omri the original enmity had been changed into a close but perhaps not quite voluntary friendship. Judah found itself drawn completely into the train of the more powerful neighbouring state, and seems even to have rendered it military service. The fall of the house of Omri was an ominous event for Judah as well as Israel; Jehu, as he passed to the throne, put to death not only Ahaziah the king but also two and forty other members of the royal house of David who had fallen into his hands; and those who still survived, children for the most part, were murdered wholesale by the regent Athaliah for reasons that are unknown. Only one little boy, Joash, was concealed from her fury, and by a successful conspiracy six years afterwards was placed upon the throne of his ancestors. At that time the Syrians were extending their incursions to Judah and Philistia, and Joash bought them off from Jerusalem with the temple treasures. Perhaps it was this disgrace that he expiated with his death; in like manner perhaps the assassination of his successor Amaziah is to be accounted for by the discredit he had incurred by a reckless and unsuccessful war against Israel. Just as Israel was beginning to recover itself after the happy termination of the Syrian wars, Judah also experienced its period of highest prosperity. What Jeroboam II. was to the northern kingdom, Uzziah was to that of the south. He appears to have obtained possession of Edom, and for a considerable time to have held that one province of David's conquests which fell to Judah. At the trading port of Elath he revived the commerce which Solomon had created. The prosperity of his long reign was uninterrupted till in his later years he was smitten with leprosy, and found it necessary to hand over the affairs of the kingdom to his son Jotham. But Jotham appears to have died about the same time as his father,— his successor, still in very early youth (Isa. iii. 12), being Ahaz ben Jotham ben Uzziah.

If Judah could not compare with Israel in political and general historical importance, it nevertheless enjoyed more than one considerable advantage over the larger kingdom. It was much safer from foreign foes; for the Egyptians, as a rule, were not dangerous neighbours. But its chief advantage consisted in the stability of its dynasty. It was David who had elevated Judah and Jerusalem to a position of historical significance, and the prosperity of his house was most intimately connected with that of the town and territory, and even with that of religion. On two separate occasions it occurred that a king of Judah was murdered by subjects, but in both cases the "people of the land" rose up against the assassins and once more placed a member of the Davidic family upon the throne. The one actual recorded revolution was that against Athaliah, which had for its object the restoration of the throne to the legitimate heir. Under shelter of the monarchy the other institutions of the state also acquired a measure of permanency such as was not found at all in Israel, where everything depended on the character of individuals, and the existing order of things was ever liable to be subjected to fresh dispute. Life in Judah was a much more stable affair, though not so exciting or dramatic. Possibly the greater isolation of the little kingdom, its more intimate relations with the neighbouring wilderness, and the more primitive modes of life which resulted, were also factors which contributed to this general result.

In the capital of course the life was not primitive, and its influence was undoubtedly greater than that of the country. Successive kings exerted themselves for its external improvement, and in this respect Hezekiah ben Ahaz was specially distinguished. Above all they manifested great interest in the temple, which from an early period exerted a powerful force of attraction over the entire mass of the population. They regulated the cultus according to their individual tastes, added to it or curtailed it at their pleasure, and dealt with the sacred treasures as they chose. Although the priests had in a certain sense great power—the conspiracy against Athaliah was led not by a prophet but by a priest—they were nevertheless subjects of the king, and had to act according to his orders. That the cultus of Jehovah at Jerusalem was purer than that at Bethel or at Samaria is an assertion which is contradicted by more than one well-attested fact. In this respect there was no essential difference between Israel and Judah. It was in Israel that the reaction against Baal-worship originated which afterwards passed over into Judah; the initiative in all such matters was Israel's. There the experiments were made from which Jerusalem learned the lesson. How deep was the interest felt in the affairs of the larger kingdom by the inhabitants even of one of the smaller provincial towns of Judah is shown in the instance of Amos of Tekoa.

Step by step with the decline of Israel after the death of Jeroboam II. did Judah rise in importance; it was already preparing to take the inheritance.

The man through whom the transition of the history from Israel to Judah was effected, and who was the means of securing for the latter kingdom a period of respite, which was fruitful of the best results for the consolidation of true religion, was the prophet Isaiah. The history of his activity is at the same time the history of Judah during that period.

Isaiah became conscious of his vocation in the year of King Uzziah's death; his earliest discourses date from the beginning of the reign of Ahaz. In them he contemplates the imminent downfall of Samaria, and threatens Judah also with the chastisement its political and social sins deserve. In chap. ix., and also in chaps. ii.–v., he still confines himself on the whole to generalities quite after the manner of Amos. But on the occasion of the expedition of the allied Syrians and Ephraimites against Jerusalem he interposed with bold decision in the sphere of practical politics. To the very last he endeavoured to restrain Ahaz from his purpose of summoning the Assyrians to his help; he assured him of Jehovah's countenance, and offered him a token in pledge. When the king refused this, the prophet recognised that matters had gone too far, and that the coming of the Assyrians could not be averted. He then declared that the dreaded danger would indeed be obviated by that course, but that another far more serious would be incurred. For the Egyptians would resist the westward movement of Assyria, and Judah, as the field of war, would be utterly laid waste; only a remnant would remain as the basis of a better future.

The actual issue, however, was not yet quite so disastrous. The Egyptians did not interfere with the Assyrians, and left Samaria and Damascus to their fate. Judah became indeed tributary to Assyria, but at the same time enjoyed considerable prosperity. Henceforward the prophet's most zealous efforts were directed to the object of securing the maintenance, at any price, of this condition of affairs. He sought by every means at his command to keep Judah from any sort of intervention in the politics of the great powers, in order that it might devote itself with undivided energies to the necessities of internal affairs. He actually succeeded in maintaining the peace for many years, even at times when in the petty kingdoms around the spirit of revolt was abroad. The ill success of all attempts elsewhere to shake off the yoke confirmed him in the conviction that Assyria was the rod of chastisement wielded by Jehovah over the nations, who had no alternative but to yield to its iron sway.

While thirty years passed thus peacefully away so far as foreign relations were concerned, internal changes of all the greater importance were taking place. Hezekiah ben Ahaz undertook for the first time a thoroughgoing reformation in the cultus of Jehovah. " He removed the high places, and brake the pillars, and cut down the Asherah, and brake in pieces the brazen serpent that Moses had made;" so we are told in 2 Kings xviii. 4, with a mixture of the general and the special that does not inspire much confidence. For, *e.g.*, the "high places" which Solomon had raised on the Mount of Olives were not removed by Hezekiah, although they stood quite close to Jerusalem, and moreover were consecrated to foreign deities. And in every respect there must have been a wide difference between the objects and results of the reformations of Hezekiah and Josiah. Undoubtedly Hezekiah undertook his reforms in worship under the influence of Isaiah. Following in the footsteps of Hosea, who had been the first to take and to express offence at the use of images in the worship of Jehovah, this prophet, utilising the impression which the destruction of Samaria had produced in Jerusalem (Isa. xvii., *cf.* Jer. iii.), strove to the utmost against the adoration of the work of men's hands in the holy places, against the Asherahs and pillars (sun-pillars), and, above all, against the ephods, *i.e.*, the idols of silver and gold, of which the land was full. But against the high places in and by themselves, against the multiplicity of the altars of Jehovah, he made no protest. "(In the Messianic time) ye shall loathe and cast away as an unclean thing your graven images with silver coverings and your molten images overlaid with gold," he says (xxx. 22); and the inference is that he contemplated the purification of the high places from superstitious excesses, but by no means their abolition. To this one object[1] Hezekiah's reformation seems to have confined itself—an object of much greater primary importance than the destruction of the altars themselves. Their destruction was a measure which arose simply out of despair of the possibility of cleansing them.

Sargon, king of Assyria, was succeeded in 705 by Sennacherib. The opportunity was seized by Merodach Baladan of Babylon to secure his independence; and by means of an embassy he urged Hezekiah also to throw off the yoke. The proposal was adopted, and the king of Judah was joined by other petty kingdoms, especially some of the Philistine towns. Relations with Egypt were established to secure its support in case of need. Sennacherib's more immediate and pressing business in Babylon enabled Palestine to gain some time; but the issue of that revolt made self-deception impossible as to the probable result of the other movement.

This was the period at which Isaiah, already far advanced in life, wielded his greatest influence. The

[1] That is, to the abolition of the images. Jeremiah's polemic is directed no longer against the images, but against wood and stone, *i.e.*, Asherahs and pillars. The date of the reformation under Hezekiah is uncertain; perhaps it ought to be placed after Sennacherib's withdrawal from Jerusalem.

preparations for revolt, the negotiations with Egypt, were concealed from him—a proof how greatly he was feared at court. When he came to know of them, it was already too late to undo what had been done. But he could at least give vent to his anger. With Jerusalem, it seemed to him, the story of Samaria was repeating itself; uninstructed by that sad lesson, the capital was giving itself up to the mad intoxication of leaders who would inevitably bring her to ruin. " Quietness and rest" had been the motto given by Jehovah to Judah, powerless as it was and much in need of a period of peace; instead of this, defiance based on ignorance and falsehood expressed the prevailing temper. But those who refused to listen to the intelligible language of Jehovah would be compelled to hear Him speak in Assyrian speech in a way that would deafen and blind them. Isaiah shows himself no less indignant against the crowd that stupidly stared at his excitement than against the God-forsaken folly of the king, with his counsellors, his priests, and his prophets. They do not suffer themselves to be shaken out of their ordinary routine by the gravity of such a crisis as this; the living work of Jehovah is to them a sealed book; their piety does not extend beyond the respect they show for certain human precepts learnt by rote.

Meanwhile Sennacherib, at the head of a great army, was advancing against Philistia and Judah along the Phœnician coast (701). Having captured Ascalon, he next laid siege to Ekron, which, after the Egyptian army sent to its relief had been defeated at Eltekeh, fell into the enemy's hand, and was severely dealt with. Simultaneously various fortresses of Judah were occupied, and the level country was devastated (Isa. i.). The consequence was that Hezekiah, in a state of panic, offered to the Assyrians his submission, which was accepted on payment of a heavy penalty, he being permitted, however, to retain possession of Jerusalem. He seemed to have got cheaply off from the unequal contest.

The way being thus cleared, Sennacherib pressed on southwards, for the Egyptians were collecting their forces against him. The nearer he came to the enemy the more undesirable did he find it that he should leave in his rear so important a fortress as Jerusalem in the hands of a doubtful vassal. Notwithstanding the recently ratified treaty, therefore, he demanded the surrender of the city, believing that a policy of intimidation would be enough to secure it from Hezekiah. But there was another personality in Jerusalem of whom his plans had taken no account. Isaiah had indeed regarded the revolt from Assyria as a rebellion against Jehovah Himself, and therefore as a perfectly hopeless undertaking, which could only result in the utmost humiliation and sternest chastisement for Judah. But much more distinctly than Amos and Hosea before him did he hold firm as an article of faith the conviction that the kingdom would not be utterly annihilated; all his speeches of solemn warning closed with the announcement that a remnant should return and form the kernel of a new commonwealth to be fashioned after Jehovah's own heart. For him, in contrast to Amos, the great crisis had a positive character; in contrast to Hosea, he did not expect a temporary suspension of the theocracy, to be followed by its complete reconstruction, but in the pious and God-fearing individuals who were still to be met with in this Sodom of iniquity, he saw the threads, thin, indeed, yet sufficient, which formed the links between the Israel of the present and its better future. Over against the vain confidence of the multitude Isaiah had hitherto brought into prominence the darker obverse of his religious belief, but now he confronted their present depression with its bright reverse; faint-heartedness was still more alien to his nature than temerity. In the name of Jehovah he bade King Hezekiah be of good courage, and urged that he should by no means surrender. The Assyrians would not be able to take the city, not even to shoot an arrow into it, nor to bring up their siege train against it. "I know thy sitting, thy going, and thy standing," is Jehovah's language to the Assyrian, "and also thy rage against Me. And I will put my ring in thy nose, and my bridle

THE DELIVERANCE OF JUDAH. 105

in thy lips, and I will turn thee back by the way by which thou camest." And thus it proved in the issue. By a still unexplained catastrophe, the main army of Sennacherib was annihilated on the frontier between Egypt and Palestine, and Jerusalem thereby freed from all danger. The Assyrian king had to save himself by a hurried retreat to Nineveh; Isaiah was triumphant. A more magnificent close of a period of influential public life can hardly be imagined.

(What Sennacherib himself relates of his expedition against his rebellious vassals in Palestine[1] runs parallel with 2 Kings xviii. 14–16, but not with the rest of the Bible narrative. These three verses are peculiar, and their source is different from that of the context. After having captured various Phœnician cities, and received tribute from a number of kings, his first measure is forcibly to restore the Assyrian governor who had been expelled from Ascalon, and next he turns his arms against Ekron. This city had put in irons its own king, Padi (who remained loyal to the suzerain), and handed him over to Hezekiah, who appears as the soul of the rebellion in these quarters. The Egyptians, who as usual have a hand in the matter, advance with an army for the relief of the beleaguered city, but are defeated near Eltekeh in the immediate neighbourhood; Ekron is taken, remorselessly chas-

[1] George Smith, "Assyrian Eponym Canon," pp. 67, 68, 131-136.

tised, and forced to take Padi back again as its king. For Hezekiah in the meantime has delivered up his prisoner, and, terrified by the fall of his fortresses and the devastation of his territory, has accepted the position of a vassal once more, paying at the same time a heavy fine, inclusive of thirty talents of gold and 800 of silver. Such is the Assyrian account. If we treat the 300 talents mentioned in 2 Kings xviii. 14 as Syrian (= 800 Babylonian), it completely fills in the vague outlines given in 2 Kings xviii. 14–16, and, while confirming in their place immediately after ver. 13 these verses, unrelated as they are to the main connection of the Biblical narrative, corrects them only in one point, by making it probable that the subjection of Hezekiah (which is not equivalent to the surrender of his city) took place while Sennacherib was still before Ekron, and not at later date when he had gone further south towards Libnah. As regards his further advance towards Egypt, and the reasons of his sudden withdrawal (related by Herodotus also from Egyptian tradition), the great king is silent, having nothing to boast of in it. The battle of Eltekeh, which is to be regarded only as an episode in the siege of Ekron, being merely the repulse of the Egyptian relieving army, was not an event of great historical importance, and ought not to be brought into any connection either with 2 Kings xix. 7 or with xix. 35; Sennacherib's inscription speaks only of the first and prosperous stage of the expedition, not of the decisive one which resulted so disastrously for him, as must be clear from the words themselves to every unprejudiced reader.)

CHAPTER VIII.

THE PROPHETIC REFORMATION.

ISAIAH was so completely a prophet that even his wife was called the prophetess after him. No such title could have been bestowed on the wife of either Amos or Hosea. But what distinguished him more than anything else from those predecessors was that his position was not, like theirs, apart from the government; he sat close to the helm, and took a very real part in directing the course of the vessel. He was more positive and practical than they; he wished to make his influence felt, and when for the moment he was unsuccessful in this so far as the great whole of the state was concerned, he busied himself in gathering round him a small circle of like-minded persons on whom his hope for the future rested. Now that Israel had been destroyed, he wished at all events to save Judah. The lofty ideality of his faith (ii. 1 *seq.*) did not hinder him from calling in the aid of practical means for this end. But the current of his activities was by the circumstances of the case directed into a channel

THE PROPHETIC REFORMATION. 109

in which after his death they continued to flow towards a goal which had hardly been contemplated by himself.

The political importance of the people of Jehovah was reduced to a minimum when Judah only was left. Already at an earlier period in that kingdom the sacred had come to be of more importance than the secular; much more was this the case under the suzerainty of Assyria. The circumstances of the time themselves urged that the religion of Israel should divest itself of all politico-national character; but Isaiah also did his best to further this end. It was his most zealous endeavour to hold king and people aloof from every patriotic movement; to him the true religious attitude was one of quietness and sitting still, non-intervention in political affairs, concentration on the problems of internal government. But he was compelled to leave over for the coming Messiah (xi. 1 *seq.*) that reformation in legal and social matters which seemed to him so necessary; all that he could bring the secular rulers of his country to undertake was a reform in worship. This was the most easily solved of the problems alluded to above, and it was also that which most closely corresponded to the character of the kingdom of Judah. Thus it came about that the reform of the theocracy which had been contemplated by Isaiah led to its transformation into an ecclesiastical state. No less influential in effecting a radical change in the old popular religion was Isaiah's doctrine which identified the true Israel with the holy remnant which alone should emerge from the crisis unconsumed. For that remnant was more than a mere object of hope; it actually stood before him in the persons of that little group of pious individuals gathered around him. Isaiah founded no "*ecclesiola in ecclesia*" indeed, but certainly an "*ecclesia in civitate Dei.*" Now began that distinction between the true Israel and the Israel according to the flesh, that bipartite division of the nation which became so important in later times. As head and founder of the prophetic party in Judah, Isaiah was, involuntarily, the man who took the first steps towards the institution of the Church.

The catastrophe which befell the army of Sennacherib had no very great effect upon the external affairs of Judah. Sennacherib indeed, being busy in the east, was unable to retrieve the loss he had sustained, but his son Esarhaddon, who succeeded him in 681, resumed the Egyptian war with better success. He made himself master of the Nile valley, and brought the Ethiopians into submission. That the petty kingdoms of Palestine returned to the old relations of dependence is to be taken as a matter of course. Judah appears to have resumed the yoke voluntarily. It appears to have made but little impression, that Manasseh ben Hezekiah came again under Assyrian suzerainty; since the time of Ahaz Judah had been accustomed to this relation. The Book of Kings speaks only of internal affairs under the reign of Manasseh. According to it, he was a bad ruler, who permitted, and even caused innocent blood to flow like water. But what was of greater consequence for the future, he took up an attitude of hostility towards the prophetic party of reform, and put himself on the side of the reaction which would fain bring back to the place of honour the old popular half-pagan conception of Jehovah, as against the pure and holy God whom the prophets worshipped. The revulsion manifested itself as the reform had done, chiefly in matters of worship. The old idolatrous furniture of the sanctuaries was reinstated in its place, and new frippery was imported from all quarters, especially from Assyria and Babylon, to renovate the old religion; with Jehovah was now associated a "queen of heaven." Yet, as usual, the restoration did more than merely bring back the old order of things. What at an earlier period had been mere naïveté now became superstition, and could hold its ground only by having imparted to it artificially a deeper meaning which was itself borrowed from the prophetical circle of ideas. Again, earnestness superseded the old joyousness of the cultus; this now had reference principally to sin and its atonement. Value was attached to services rendered to the Deity, just in proportion to their hardness and unnaturalness; at this period it was that the old precept to sacrifice to Jehovah the male that opens the matrix was extended to children. The counter-reformation was far from being unaffected by the preceding reformation, although it understood religious earnestness in quite another sense, and sought, not to eliminate heathenism from the cultus, but to animate it with new life. On the other hand, the reaction was, in the end, found to have left distinct traces of its influence in the ultimate issue of the reformation.

We possess one document dating from Manasseh's time in Micah vi. 1–vii. 6. Here, where the lawlessness and utter disregard of every moral restraint in Judah are set in a hideous light, the prophetic point of view, as contrasted with the new refinements in worship, attains also its simplest and purest expression. Perhaps to this period the Decalogue also, which is so eloquently silent in regard to cultus, is to be assigned. Jehovah demands nothing for Himself, all that He asks is only for men; this is here the fundamental law of the theocracy.

Manasseh's life was a long one, and his son Amon walked in his ways. The latter died after a brief reign, and with his death a new era for Judah began. It was introduced by the great catastrophe in which the Assyrian empire came to an end. The sovereignty of the world was beginning to pass out

THE PROPHETIC REFORMATION. 113

of the hands of the Semites into those of the Aryans. Phraortes of Media indeed was unsuccessful in his attempt against the Assyrians, but Cyaxares beat them and proceeded to besiege their capital. The Scythian invasion of Media and Western Asia (c. 630) at this juncture gave them another respite of more than twenty years; but even it tended to break in pieces the great, loosely-compacted monarchy. The provinces became gradually disintegrated, and the kingdom shrivelled up till it covered no more than the land of Asshur.[1]

The inroad of the Scythians aroused to energy again the voice of prophecy which had been dumb during the very sinful but not very animated period of Manasseh's reign. Zephaniah and Jeremiah threatened with the mysterious northern foe, just as Amos and Hosea had formerly done with the Assyrians. The Scythians actually did invade

---

[1] Our knowledge of the events of the second half of the seventh century has remained singularly imperfect hitherto, notwithstanding the importance of the changes they wrought on the face of the ancient world. The account given above is that of Herodotus (i. 103-106), and there the matter must rest until really authentic sources shall have been brought to light. With regard to the final siege of Nineveh, our chief informant is Ctesias, as quoted by Diodorus (ii. 26, 27). Whether the prophecy of Nahum relates to the *last* siege is doubtful (in spite of ii. 7, and the oracle given in Diodorus, ὅτι τὴν Νίνον οὐδεὶς ἐλεῖ κατὰ κράτος ἐὰν μὴ πρότερον ὁ ποταμὸς τῇ πόλει γένηται πολέμιος), inasmuch as Nahum (i. 9) expressly speaks of the siege alluded to by him as the first, saying, "the trouble shall not rise up the second time."

Palestine in 626 (the 13th year of Josiah), and penetrated as far as to Egypt; but their course lay along the shore line, and they left Judah untouched. This danger that had come so near and yet passed them by, this instance of a prophetic threatening that had come to pass and yet been mercifully averted, made a powerful impression upon the people of Judah; public opinion went through a revolution in favour of the reforming party which was able to gain for itself the support also of the young king Josiah ben Amon. The circumstances were favourable for coming forward with a comprehensive programme for a reconstruction of the theocracy. In the year 621 (the eighteenth of Josiah) Deuteronomy was discovered, accepted, and carried into effect.

The Deuteronomic legislation is designed for the reformation, by no means of the cultus alone, but at least quite as much of the civil relations of life. The social interest is placed above the cultus, inasmuch as everywhere humane ends are assigned for the rites and offerings. In this it is plainly seen that Deuteronomy is the progeny of the prophetic spirit. Still more plainly does this appear in the *motifs* of the legislation; according to these, Jehovah is the only God, whose service demands the whole heart and every energy; He has entered into a covenant with Israel, but upon fundamental conditions that, as contained in the Decalogue, are purely moral and of absolute universality. Nowhere does the fundamental religious thought of prophecy find clearer expression than in Deuteronomy,—the thought that Jehovah asks nothing for Himself, but asks it as a religious duty that man should render to man what is right, that His will lies not in any unknown height, but in the moral sphere which is known and understood by all.[1]

But the result of the innovation did not correspond exactly to its prophetic origin. Prophecy died when its precepts attained to the force of laws; the prophetic ideas lost their purity when they became practical. Whatever may have been contemplated, only provisional regulations actually admitted of being carried, and even these only in co-operation with the king and the priests, and with due regard to the capacity of the masses. The final outcome of the Deuteronomic reformation was principally that the cultus of Jehovah was limited to Jerusalem and abolished everywhere else,—such was the popular and practical form of prophetic monotheism. The importance of the Solomonic temple

[1] The commandments which I command thee are not unattainable for thee, neither are they far off; not in heaven so that one might say, Who can climb up into heaven and bring them down, and tell us them that we might do them! not beyond the sea so that one might say, Who shall go over the sea, and fetch them, and tell us them that we might do them!—but the matter lies very near thee, in thy mouth and in thy heart, so that thou canst do it (Deut. xxx. 11–14).

was thereby increased in the highest degree, and so also the influence of the priests of Jerusalem, the sons of Zadok, who now in point of fact got rid entirely of their rivals, the priests of the country districts.

CHAPTER IX.

JEREMIAH AND THE DESTRUCTION OF JERUSALEM.

JOSIAH lived for thirteen years after the accomplishment of his great work. It was a happy period of external and internal prosperity. The nation possessed the covenant, and kept it. It seemed as if the conditions had been attained on which, according to the prophets, the continuance of the theocracy depended; if their threatenings against Israel had been fulfilled, so now was Judah proving itself the heir of their promises. Already in Deuteronomy is the "extension of the frontier" taken into consideration, and Josiah actually put his hand to the task of seeking the attainment of this end.

Jehovah and Israel, religion and patriotism, once more went hand in hand. Jeremiah alone did not suffer himself to be misled by the general feeling. He was a second Amos, upon a higher platform— but, unlike his predecessor, a prophet by profession; his history, like Isaiah's, is practically the history of his time. In the work of introducing Deuteronomy he had taken an active part, and throughout his life he showed his zeal against unlawful altars and against the adoration of wood and stone (Asherahs and pillars). But he was by no means satisfied with the results of the reformation that had been effected; nothing appeared to him more sinful or more silly than the false confidence produced by it in Jehovah and in the inviolability of His one true temple. This confidence he maintained to be delusive; Judah was not a whit better than Israel had been, the temple of Jerusalem would be destroyed one day like the temple of Shiloh. The external improvements on which the people of Judah prided themselves he held to leave this severe judgment unaffected; what was needed was a quite different sort of change, a change of heart, not very easy positively to define.

An opportunity for showing his opposition presented itself to the prophet at the juncture when King Josiah had fallen at Megiddo in the battle with Pharaoh Necho (608), and when the people were seeking safety and protection by cleaving to Jehovah and His holy temple. At the instance of the priests and the prophets he had almost expiated with his blood the blasphemies he had uttered against the popular belief; but he did not suffer himself to be driven from his course. Even when the times had grown quiet again, he persisted, at the risk of his life and under universal reproach and ridicule, in his work as a prophet of evil. Moments of despair sometimes came to him; but that he had correctly estimated the true value of the great conversion of the nation was speedily proved by the facts. Although Deuteronomy was not formally abolished under Jehoiakim, who as the vassal of Egypt ascended the throne of his father Josiah, nevertheless it ceased to have practical weight, the battle of Megiddo having shown that in spite of the covenant with Jehovah the possibilities of nonsuccess in war remained the same as before. Jehoiakim tended to return to the ways of Manasseh, not only as regarded idolatry, but also in his contempt for law and the private rights of his subjects; —the two things seem to stand in connection.

The course of events at last brought upon the theocracy the visible ruin which Jeremiah had been so long expecting. After the Egyptians had subjugated Syria at the time when the Medes and Chaldæans were busied with the siege of Nineveh, Nebuchadnezzar, that task accomplished, came upon them from Babylon and routed them on the Euphrates near Carchemish (605–4). The people of Judah rejoiced at the fall of Nineveh, and also at the result of Carchemish; but they were soon undeceived when the prospect began to open on them of simply exchanging the Egyptian for the Chaldæan yoke. The power of the Chaldæans had been quite unsuspected, and now it was found that in them the

Assyrians had suddenly returned to life. Jeremiah was the only man who gained any credit by these events. His much ridiculed "enemy out of the north," of whom he had of old been wont to speak so much, now began to be talked of with respect, although his name was no longer "the Scythian" but "the Babylonian." It was an epoch,—the close of an account which balanced in his favour. Therefore it was that precisely at this moment he received the Divine command to commit to writing that which for twenty-three years he had been preaching, and which, ever pronounced impossible, had now showed itself so close at hand.

After the victory of Carchemish the Chaldæans drove Pharaoh out of Syria, and also compelled the submission of Jehoiakim (c. 602). For three years he continued to pay his tribute, and then he withheld it; a mad passion for liberty, kindled by religious fanaticism, had begun to rage with portentous power amongst the influential classes, the grandees, the priests, and the prophets. Nebuchadnezzar satisfied himself in the first instance with raising against Judah several of the smaller nationalities around, especially the Edomites; not till 597 did he appear in person before Jerusalem. The town was compelled to yield; the more important citizens were carried into exile, amongst them the young king Jechoniah, son of Jehoiakim, who had died in the interval; Zedekiah ben Josiah was made king in his stead over the remnant left behind. The patriotic fanaticism that had led to the revolt was not broken even by this blow. Within four years afterwards new plans of liberation began to be again set on foot; on this occasion, however, the influence of Jeremiah proved strong enough to avert the danger. But when a definite prospect of help from Pharaoh Hophra (Apries) presented itself in 589, the craving for independence proved quite irrepressible. Revolt was declared; and in a very short time the Chaldæan army, with Nebuchadnezzar at its head, lay before Jerusalem. For a while everything seemed to move prosperously; the Egyptians came to the rescue, and the Chaldæans were compelled to raise the siege in order to cope with them. At this there was great joy in Jerusalem; only Jeremiah continued to express his gloomy views. The event proved that he was right; the Egyptians were repulsed and the siege resumed. The city was bent on obstinate resistance; in vain did Jeremiah, at continual risk of his life, endeavour to bring it to reason. The king, who agreed with the prophet, did not venture to assert his opinion against the dominant terrorism. The town in these circumstances was at last taken by storm, and, along with the temple, reduced to ruins. Cruel vengeance was taken on the king and grandees, and the pacification of the country was ensured by another and larger deportation of the inhabitants to Babylon. Thus terminated in 586 the kingdom of Judah.

The prophets had been the spiritual destroyers of the old Israel. In old times the nation had been the ideal of religion in actual realisation; the prophets confronted the nation with an ideal to which it did not correspond. Then to bridge over this interval the abstract ideal was framed into a law, and to this law the nation was to be conformed. The attempt had very important consequences, inasmuch as Jehovah continued to be a living power in the law, when He was no longer realised as present in the nation; but that was not what the prophets had meant to effect. What they were unconsciously labouring towards was that religious individualism which had its historical source in the national downfall, and manifested itself not exclusively within the prophetical sphere. With such men as Amos and Hosea the moral personality based upon an inner conviction burst through the limits of mere nationality; their mistake was in supposing that they could make their way of thinking the basis of a national life. Jeremiah saw through the mistake; the true Israel was narrowed to himself. Of the truth of his conviction he never had a moment's doubt; he knew that Jehovah was on his side, that on him depended the eternal future. Instead of the nation, the heart and the individual conviction were to him the subject of religion. On the ruins of Jerusalem he gazed into the future filled with joyful hope, sure of this, that Jehovah would one day pardon past sin and renew the relation which had been broken off—though on the basis of another covenant than that laid down in Deuteronomy. "I will put my law upon their heart, and write it on their mind; none shall say to his neighbour, Know the Lord, for all shall have that knowledge within them."

CHAPTER X.

THE CAPTIVITY AND THE RESTORATION.

THE exiled Jews were not scattered all over Chaldæa, but were allowed to remain together in families and clans. Many of them, notwithstanding this circumstance, must have lapsed and become merged in the surrounding heathenism; but many also continued faithful to Jehovah and to Israel. They laboured under much depression and sadness, groaning under the wrath of Jehovah, who had rejected His people and cancelled His covenant. They were lying under a sort of vast interdict; they could not celebrate any sacrifice or keep any feast; they could only observe days of fasting and humiliation, and such rites as had no inseparable connection with the Holy Land. The observance of the Sabbath, and the practice of the rite of circumcision, acquired much greater importance than they formerly possessed as signs of a common religion. The meetings on the Sabbath day out of which the synagogues were afterwards developed appear to have first come into use during this period; perhaps also even then it had become customary to read aloud from the prophetic writings which set forth that all had happened in the providence of God, and moreover that the days of adversity were not to last for ever.

Matters improved somewhat as Cyrus entered upon his victorious career. Was he the man in whom the Messianic prophecies had found their fulfilment? The majority were unwilling to think so. For it was out of Israel (they argued) that the Messiah was to proceed who should establish the kingdom of God upon the ruins of the kingdoms of the world; the restitution effected by means of a Persian could only be regarded as a passing incident in the course of an historical process that had its goal entirely elsewhere. This doubt was met by more than one prophetical writer, and especially by the great anonymous author to whom we are indebted for Isa. xl., *seq.* "Away with sorrow; deliverance is already at the door! Is it then a humiliating thing that Israel should owe its freedom to a Persian? Nay, is it not rather a proof of the world-wide sway of the God of Jacob that He should thus summon His instruments from the ends of the earth? Who else than Jehovah could have thus sent Cyrus? Surely not the false gods which He has destroyed? Jehovah alone it was who foretold and foreknew the things which are now coming to pass,—because long ago He had prearranged and predetermined them, and they are now being executed in accordance with His plan. Rejoice therefore in prospect of your near deliverance; prepare yourselves for the new era; gird yourselves for the return to your homes." It is to be observed, as characteristic in this prophecy, how the idea of Jehovah as God alone and God over all—in constantly recurring lyrical parenthesis He is praised as the author of the world and of all nature—is yet placed in positive relation to Israel alone, and that upon the principle that Israel is in exclusive possession of the universal truth, which cannot perish with Israel, but must, through the instrumentality of Israel, become the common possession of the whole world. "There is no God but Jehovah, and Israel is His prophet."

For many years the Persian monarch put the patience of the Jews to the proof; Jehovah's judgment upon the Chaldæans, instead of advancing, seemed to recede. At length, however, their hopes were realised; in the year 538 Cyrus brought the empire of Babylon to an end, and gave the exiles leave to seek their fatherland once more. This permission was not made use of by all, or even by a majority. The number of those who returned is stated at 42,360; whether women and children are included in this figure is uncertain. On arriving at their destination, after the difficult march through the desert, they did not spread themselves over the whole of Judah, but settled chiefly in the neighbourhood of Jerusalem. The Calebites, for example, who previously had had their settlements in and around Hebron, now settled in Bethlehem and in the district of Ephrath. They found it necessary to concentrate themselves in face of a threatened admixture of doubtful elements. From all sides people belonging to the surrounding nations had pressed into the depopulated territory of Judah. Not only had they annexed the border territories—where, for example, the Edomites or Idumæans held the whole of the Negeb as far as to Hebron; they had effected lodgments everywhere, and—as the Ammonites, Ashdodites, and especially the Samaritans—had amalgamated with the older Jewish population, a residue of which had remained in the country in spite of all that had happened. These half-breed " pagani " (Amme haareç) gave a friendly reception to the returning exiles (Bne haggola); particularly did the Samaritans show themselves anxious to make common cause with them. But they were met with no reciprocal cordiality. The lesson of religious isolation which the children of the captivity had learned in Babylon, they did not forget on their return to their home. Here also they lived as in a strange land. Not the native of Judæa, but the man who could trace his descent from the exiles in Babylon, was reckoned as belonging to their community.

The first decennia after the return of the exiles, during which they were occupied in adjusting themselves to their new homes, were passed under a variety of adverse circumstances, and by no means either in joyousness or security. Were these then the Messianic times which, it had been foretold, were to dawn at the close of their captivity? They did not, at all events, answer the expectations which had been formed. A settlement had been again obtained, it was true, in the Fatherland; but the Persian yoke pressed now more heavily than ever the Babylonian had done. The sins of God's people seemed still unforgiven, their period of bond-service not yet at an end. A slight improvement, as is shown by the prophecies of Haggai and Zechariah, followed, when in the year 520 the obstacles disappeared, which until then had stood in the way of the rebuilding of the temple; the work then begun was completed in 516. Inasmuch as the Jews were now nothing more than a religious community, based upon the traditions of a national existence that had ceased, the rebuilding of the temple naturally was for them an event of supreme importance.

The law of the new theocracy was the Book of Deuteronomy; this was the foundation on which the structure was to be built. But the force of circumstances and the spirit of the age had even before and during the exile exerted a modifying influence upon that legislative code; and it continued to do so still. At first a "son of David" had continued to stand at the head of the Bne haggola, but this last relic of the old monarchy soon had to give way to the Persian governor, who was under the control of the satrap of trans-Euphratic Syria, and whose principal business was the collection of revenue. Thenceforward the sole national chief was Joshua, the high priest, on whom, accordingly, the political representation also of the community naturally devolved. In the circumstances as they then were no other arrangement was possible. The way had been paved for it long before, in so far as the Assyrians had destroyed the kingdom of Israel, while in the kingdom of Judah, which survived it, the religious cultus had greater importance attached to it than political affairs, and also inasmuch as in point of fact the practical issue of the prophetic reformation sketched in Deuteronomy had been to make the temple the national centre still more than formerly. The hierocracy towards which Ezekiel had already opened the way was simply inevitable. It took the form of a monarchy of the high priest, he having stepped into the place formerly occupied by the theocratic king. As his peers and at his side stood the members of his clan, the Levites of the old Jerusalem, who traced their descent from Zadok (Sadduk); the common Levites held a much lower rank, so far as they had maintained their priestly rank at all and had not been degraded, in accordance with Ezekiel's law (chap. xliv.), to the position of mere temple servitors. "Levite," once the title of honour bestowed on all priests, became more and more confined to members of the second order of the clergy.

Meanwhile no improvement was taking place in the condition of the Jewish colonists. They were poor; they had incurred the hostility of their neighbours by their exclusiveness; the Persian Government was suspicious; the incipient decline of the great kingdom was accompanied with specially unpleasant consequences so far as Palestine was concerned (Megabyzus). All this naturally tended to produce in the community a certain laxity and depression. To what purpose (it was asked) all this religious strictness, which led to so much that was unpleasant? Why all this zeal for Jehovah, who refused to be mollified by it? It is a significant fact that the upper ranks of the priesthood were least of all concerned to counteract this tendency. Their priesthood was less to them than the predominance which was based upon it; they looked upon the neighbouring ethnarchs as their equals, and maintained relations of friendship with them. The general community was only following their example when it also began to mingle with the Amme haareç.

The danger of Judaism merging into heathenism was imminent. But it was averted by a new accession from without. In the year 458 Ezra the scribe, with a great number of his compatriots, set out from Babylon, for the purpose of reinforcing the Jewish element in Palestine. The Jews of Babylon were more happily situated than their Palestinian brethren, and it was comparatively easy for them to take up a separatist attitude, because they were surrounded by heathenism not partial but entire. They were no great losers from the circumstances that they were precluded from participating directly in the life of the ecclesiastical community; the Torah had long ago become separated from the people, and was now an independent abstraction following a career of its own. Babylonia was the place where a further codification of the law had been placed alongside of Deuteronomy. Ezekiel had led the way in reducing to theory and to writing the sacred praxis of his time; in this he was followed by an entire school; in their exile the Levites turned scribes. Since then Babylon continued to be the home of the Torah; and, while in Palestine itself the practice was becoming laxer, the literary study had gradually intensified the strictness and distinctive peculiarities of Judaism. And now there came to Palestine a Babylonian scribe having the law of his God in his hand, and armed with authority from the Persian king to proceed upon the basis of this law with a reformation of the community.

Ezra did not set about introducing the new law immediately on his arrival in Judæa. In the first instance, he concentrated his attention on the task of effecting a strict separation between the Bne haggola and the heathen or half-heathen inhabitants. So much he could accomplish upon the basis of Deuteronomy, but it was long before he gave publicity to the law which he himself had brought. Why he hesitated so long it is impossible to say; between the seventh and the twentieth year of Artaxerxes Longimanus (458–445 B.C.) there is a great hiatus in the narrative of the books of Ezra and Nehemiah. The main reason appears to have been that, in spite of the good will of the Persian king, Ezra had not the vigorous support of the local authorities. But this was indispensably necessary in order to secure recognition for a new law.

At last, in 445, it fell to the lot of a Jew, who also shared the views of Ezra, Nehemiah ben Hakkelejah,[1] the cupbearer and the favourite of Artaxerxes, to be sent as Persian governor to Judæa. After he had freed the community from external pressure with vigour and success, and brought it into more tolerable outward circumstances, the business of introducing the new law-book was next

[1] According to the present punctuation this name is Hakalja (Hachaljah), but such a pronunciation is inadmissible; it has no possible etymology, the language having no such word as *hakal*. The name in its correct form means, "Wait upon Jehovah."

proceeded with; in this Ezra and Nehemiah plainly acted in concert.

On the first of Tisri — the year is unfortunately not given, but it cannot have been earlier than 444 B.C.—the promulgation of the law began at a great gathering in Jerusalem; Ezra, supported by the Levites, was present. Towards the end of the month, the concluding act took place, in which the community became solemnly bound by the contents of the law. Special prominence was given to those provisions with which the people were directly concerned, particularly those which related to the dues payable by the laity to the priests.

The covenant which hitherto had rested on Deuteronomy was thus expanded into a covenant based upon the entire Pentateuch. Substantially at least Ezra's law-book, in the form in which it became the Magna Charta of Judaism in or about the year 444, must be regarded as practically identical with our Pentateuch, although many minor amendments and very considerable additions may have been made at a later date.

The character of the post-Deuteronomic legislation (Priestly Code) is chiefly marked, in its external aspects, by the immense extension of the dues payable to the priests, and by the sharp distinction made between the descendants of Aaron and the common Levites; this last feature is to be traced historically to the circumstance that after the Deuteronomic reformation the legal equality between the Levites who until then had ministered at the "high places" and the priests of the temple at Jerusalem was not *de facto* recognised. Internally, it is mainly characterised by its ideal of Levitical holiness, the way in which it everywhere surrounds life with purificatory and propitiatory ceremonies, and its prevailing reference of sacrifice to sin. Noteworthy also is the manner in which everything is regarded from the point of view of Jerusalem, a feature which comes much more boldly into prominence here than in Deuteronomy; the nation and the temple are strictly speaking identified. That externalisation towards which the prophetical movement, in order to become practical, had already been tending in Deuteronomy finally achieved its acme in the legislation of Ezra; a new artificial Israel was the result; but, after all, the old would have pleased an Amos better. At the same time it must be remembered that the kernel needed a shell. It was a necessity that Judaism should incrust itself in this manner; without those hard and ossified forms the preservation of its essential elements would have proved impossible. At a time when all nationalities, and at the same time all bonds of religion and national customs, were beginning to be broken up in the seeming cosmos and real chaos of the Græco-Roman empire, the Jews stood out like a rock in the midst of the ocean. When the natural conditions of independent nationality all failed them, they nevertheless artificially maintained it with an energy truly marvellous, and thereby preserved for themselves, and at the same time for the whole world, an eternal good.

As regards the subsequent history of the Jewish community under the Persian domination, we have almost no information. The high priest in Nehemiah's time was Eliashib, son of Joiakim and grandson of Joshua, the patriarchal head of the sons of Zadok, who had returned from Babylon; he was succeeded in the direct line by Joiada, Johanan, and Jaddua (Neh. xii. 10, 11, 22); the last-named was in office at the time of Alexander the Great (Joseph., *Ant.*, xi. 8). Palestine was the province which suffered most severely of all from the storms which marked the last days of the sinking Persian empire, and it is hardly likely that the Jews escaped their force; we know definitely, however, of only one episode, in which the Persian general Bagoses interfered in a disagreeable controversy about the high-priesthood (*cir.* 375).

To this period also (and not, as Josephus states, to the time of Alexander) belongs the constitution of the Samaritan community on an independent footing by Manasseh, a Jewish priest of rank. He was expelled from Jerusalem by Nehemiah in 432, for refusing to separate from his alien wife. He took shelter with his father-in-law Sanballat, the

Samaritan prince, who built him a temple on Mount Gerizim near Shechem, where he organised a Samaritan church and a Samaritan worship, on the Jerusalem model, and on the basis of a but slightly modified Jerusalem Pentateuch. If the Samaritans had hitherto exerted themselves to the utmost to obtain admission into the fellowship of the Jews, they henceforward were as averse to have anything to do with these as these were to have any dealings with them; the temple on Mount Gerizim was now the symbol of their independence as a distinct religious sect. For the Jews this was a great advantage, as they had no longer to dread the danger of syncretism. They could now quite confidently admit the Amme haareç into their communion, in the assurance of assimilating them without any risk of the opposite process taking place. The Judaising process began first with the country districts immediately surrounding Jerusalem, and then extended to Galilee, Philistia, and many portions of Peræa. In connection with it, the Hebrew language, which hitherto had been firmly retained by the Bne haggola, now began to yield to the Aramaic, and to hold its own only as a sacred speech.

CHAPTER XI.

THE HELLENISTIC PERIOD.

PALESTINE fell into Alexander's possession in 332; after his death it had an ample share of the troubles arising out of the partition of his inheritance. In 320 it was seized by Ptolemy I., who on a Sabbath-day took Jerusalem; but in 315 he had to give way before Antigonus. Even before the battle of Ipsus, however, he seems to have recovered possession once more, and for a century thereafter Southern Syria continued to belong to the Egyptian crown, although the Seleucidæ more than once sought to wrench it away.

In the priestly dynasty during the period of the Ptolemies, Onias I. ben Jaddua was succeeded by his son Simon I., after whom again came first his brothers Eleazar and Manasseh, and next his son Onias II.; the last-named was in his turn followed by his son Simon II., whose praises are sung by the son of Sirach (xlix. 14–16). At the side of the high priest stood the gerusia of the town of Jerusalem, as a council of state, including the higher ranks of the priesthood. The new sovereign power was at once stronger and juster than the Persian, —at least under the earlier Ptolemies; the power of the national government increased; to it was entrusted the business of raising the tribute.

As a consequence of the revolutionary changes which had taken place in the conditions of the whole East, the Jewish dispersion (diaspora) began vigorously to spread. It dated its beginning indeed from an earlier period,—from the time when the Jews had lost their land and kingdom, but yet, thanks to their religion, could not part with their nationality. They did not by any means all return from Babylon; perhaps the majority permanently settled abroad. The successors of Alexander (diadochi) fully appreciated this international element, and used it as a link between their barbarian and Hellenic populations. Everywhere they encouraged the settlement of Jews,—in Asia Minor, in Syria, and especially in Egypt. Alongside of the Palestinian there arose a Hellenistic Judaism which had its metropolis in Alexandria. Here, under Ptolemy I. and II., the Torah had already been translated into Greek, and around this sprung up a Jewish-Greek literature which soon became very extensive. At the court and in the army of the Ptolemies many Jews rose to prominent positions; everywhere they received the preference over, and everywhere they in consequence earned the hatred of, the indigenous population.

THE HELLENISTIC PERIOD. 139

After the death of Ptolemy IV. (205) Antiochus III. attained the object towards which he and his predecessors had long been vainly striving; after a war protracted with varying success through several years, he succeeded at last in incorporating Palestine with the kingdom of the Seleucidæ. The Jews took his side, less perhaps because they had become disgusted with the really sadly degenerate Egyptian rule, than because they had foreseen the issue of the contest, and preferred to attach themselves voluntarily to the winning side. In grateful acknowledgment, Antiochus confirmed and enlarged certain privileges of the "holy camp," *i.e.*, of Jerusalem (Joseph., *Ant.*, xii. 3, 3). It soon, however, became manifest that the Jews had made but a poor bargain in this exchange. Three years after his defeat at Magnesia, Antiochus III. died (187), leaving to his son Seleucus IV. an immense burden of debt, which he had incurred by his unprosperous Roman war. Seleucus, in his straits, could not afford to be over-scrupulous in appropriating money where it was to be found: he did not need to be twice told that the wealth of the temple at Jerusalem was out of all proportion to the expenses of the sacrificial service. The sacred treasure accordingly made the narrowest possible escape from being plundered; Heliodorus, who had been charged by the king to seize it, is said to have been deterred at the last moment by a heavenly vision. But the Jews derived no permanent advantage from this.

It was a priest of rank, Simon by name, who had called the attention of the king to the temple treasure; his motive had been spite against the high priest Onias III., the son and successor of Simon II. The circumstance is one indication of a melancholy process of disintegration that was at that time going on within the hierocracy. The high-priesthood, although there were exceptional cases, such as that of Simon II., was regarded less as a sacred office than as a profitable princedom; within the ranks of the priestly nobility arose envious and jealous factions; personal advancement was sought by means of the favour of the overlord, who had something to say in the making of appointments. A collateral branch of the ruling family, that of the children of Tobias, had by means of the ill-gotten wealth of Joseph ben Tobias attained to a position of ascendency, and competed in point of power with the high priest himself. It appears that the above-mentioned Simon, and his still more scandalous brother Menelaus, also belonged to the Tobiadæ, and, relying upon the support of their powerful party (Jos., *Ant.*, xii. 5, 1), cherished the purpose of securing the high-priesthood by the aid of the Syrian king.

The failure of the mission of Heliodorus was attributed by Simon to a piece of trickery on the part of Onias the high priest, who accordingly found himself called upon to make his own justification at court and to expose the intrigues of his adversary. Meanwhile Seleucus IV. died of poison (175), and Antiochus IV. Epiphanes did not confirm Onias in his dignity, but detained him in Antioch, while he made over the office to his brother Jason, who had offered a higher rent. Possibly the Tobiadæ also had something to do with this arrangement; at all events, Menelaus was at the outset the right hand of the new high priest. To secure still further the favour of the king, Jason held himself out to be an enlightened friend of the Greeks, and begged for leave to found in Jerusalem a gymnasium and an ephebeum, and to be allowed to sell to the inhabitants there the rights of citizenship in Antioch,— a request which was readily granted.

The malady which had long been incubating now reached its acute phase. Just in proportion as Hellenism showed itself friendly did it present elements of danger to Judaism. From the periphery it slowly advanced towards the centre, from the diaspora to Jerusalem, from mere matters of external fashion to matters of the most profound conviction.[1] Especially did the upper and cultivated classes of society begin to feel ashamed, in presence

[1] The Hellenising fashion is amusingly exemplified in the Grecising of the Jewish names; *e.g.*, Alcimus = Eljakim, Jason = Jesus, Joshua; Menelaus = Menahem.

of the refined Greeks, of their Jewish singularity, and to do all in their power to tone it down and conceal it. In this the priestly nobility made itself conspicuous as the most secular section of the community, and it was the high priest who took the initiative in measures which aimed at a complete Hellenising of the Jews. He outdid every one else in paganism. Once he sent a considerable present for offerings to the Tyrian Hercules on the occasion of his festival; but his messenger, ashamed to apply the money to such a purpose, set it apart for the construction of royal ships of war.

The friendship shown by Jason for the Greek king and for all that was Hellenic did not prevent Antiochus IV. from setting pecuniary considerations before all others. Menelaus, entrusted with the mission of conveying to Antioch the annual Jewish tribute, availed himself of the opportunity to promote his own personal interests by offering a higher sum for the high-priesthood, and, having otherwise ingratiated himself with the king, gained his object (171). But though nominated, he did not find it quite easy to obtain possession of the post. The Tobiadæ took his side, but the body of the people stuck to Jason, who was compelled to give way only when Syrian troops had been brought upon the scene. Menelaus had immediately, however, to encounter another difficulty, for he could not at once pay the amount of tribute which he had

promised. He helped himself so far indeed by
robbing the temple, but this landed him in new
embarrassments. Onias III., who was living out
of employment at Antioch, threatened to make
compromising revelations to the king; he was,
however, opportunely assassinated. The rage of
the people against the priestly temple-plunderer
now broke out in a rising against a certain Lysi-
machus, who at the instance of the absent Menelaus
had made further inroads upon the sacred treasury.
The Jews' defence before the king (at Tyre) on
account of this uproar resolved itself into a grievous
complaint against the conduct of Menelaus. His
case was a bad one, but money again helped him
out of his straits, and the extreme penalty of the
law fell upon his accusers.

The feelings of the Jews with reference to this
wolfish shepherd may easily be imagined. Nothing
but fear of Antiochus held them in check. Then
a report gained currency that the king had perished
in an expedition against Egypt (170); and Jason,
who meanwhile had found refuge in Ammanitis,
availed himself of the prevailing current of feeling
to resume his authority with the help of one thou-
sand men. He was not able, however, to hold the
position long, partly because he showed an unwise
vindictiveness against his enemies, partly (and
chiefly) because the rumour of the death of Antiochus
turned out to be false. The king was already, in

fact, close at hand on his return from Egypt, full of anger at an insurrection which he regarded as having been directed against himself. He inflicted severe and bloody chastisement upon Jerusalem, carried off the treasures of the temple, and restored Menelaus, placing Syrian officials at his side. Jason fled from place to place, and ultimately died in misery at Lacedæmon.

The deepest despondency prevailed in Judæa; but its cup of sorrow was not yet full. Antiochus, probably soon after his last Egyptian expedition (168), sent Apollonius with an army against Jerusalem. He fell upon the unsuspecting city, disarmed the inhabitants and demolished the walls, but on the other hand fortified Acra, and garrisoned it strongly, so as to make it a standing menace to the whole country. Having thus made his preparations, he proceeded to carry out his main instructions. All that was religiously distinctive of Judaism was to be removed; such was the will of the king. The Mosaic cultus was abolished, Sabbath observance and the rite of circumcision prohibited, all copies of the Torah confiscated and burnt. In the desecrated and partially-destroyed temple pagan ceremonies were performed, and upon the great altar of burnt-offering a small altar to Zeus Olympios was erected, on which the first offering was made on 25th Kislev 168. In the country towns also heathen altars were erected, and the Jews compelled, on pain of death, publicly to adore the false gods and to eat swine's flesh that had been sacrificed to idols.

The princes and grandees of the Jews had represented to Antiochus that the people were ripe for Hellenisation; and inasmuch as, apart from this, to reduce to uniformity the extremely motley constituents of his kingdom was a scheme that lay near his heart, he was very willing to believe them. That the very opposite was the case must of course have become quite evident very soon; but the resistance of the Jews taking the form of rebellious risings against his creatures, he fell upon the hopeless plan of coercion,—hopeless, for he could attain his end only by making all Judæa one vast graveyard. There existed indeed a pagan party; the Syrian garrison of Acra was partly composed of Jews who sold themselves to be the executioners of their countrymen. Fear also influenced many to deny their convictions; but the majority adhered firmly to the religion of their fathers. Jerusalem, the centre of the process of Hellenisation, was abandoned by its inhabitants, who made their escape to Egypt, or hid themselves in the country, in deserts and caves. The scribes in especial held fast by the law; and they were joined by the party of the Asidæans (*i.e.*, pious ones).

K

CHAPTER XII.

THE HASMONÆANS.

At first there was no thought of meeting violence with violence; as the Book of Daniel shows, people consoled themselves with thoughts of the immediate intervention of God which would occur in due time. Quite casually, without either plan or concert, a warlike opposition arose. There was a certain priest Mattathias, of the family of the Hasmonæans, a man far advanced in life, whose home was in Modein, a little country town to the west of Jerusalem. Hither also the Syrian soldiers came to put the population to a positive proof of their change of faith; they insisted upon Mattathias leading the way. But he was steadfast in his refusal; and, when another Jew addressed himself before his eyes to the work of making the heathen offering, he killed him and the Syrian officer as well, and destroyed the altar. Thereupon he fled to the hill country, accompanied by his sons (Johannes Gaddi, Simon Thassi, Judas Maccabæus, Eleazar Auaran, Jonathan Apphus) and other followers. But he resolved to defend himself to the last, and not to act as some other fugitives had done, who about the same time had allowed themselves to be surrounded and butchered on a Sabbath-day without lifting a finger. Thus he became the head of a band which defended the ancestral religion with the sword. They traversed the country, demolished the altars of the false gods, circumcised the children, and persecuted the heathen and heathenishly disposed. The sect of the Asidæans also intrusted itself to their warlike protection (1 Macc. ii. 42).

Mattathias soon died and left his leadership to Judas Maccabæus, by whom the struggle was carried on in the first instance after the old fashion; soon, however, it assumed larger dimensions, when regular armies were sent out against the insurgents. First Apollonius, the governor of Judæa, took the field; but he was defeated and fell in battle. Next came Seron, governor of Cœlesyria, who also was routed near Bethhoron (166). Upon this Lysias, the regent to whom Antiochus IV., who was busied in the far east, had intrusted the government of Syria and the charge of his son, Antiochus Philopator, a minor, sent a strong force under the command of three generals. Approaching from the west, it was their design to advance separately upon Jerusalem, but Judas anticipated their plan and compelled them to quit the field (166). The regent now felt himself called on to interpose in person.

Invading Judæa from the south, he encountered the Jews at Bethsur, who, however, offered an opposition that was not easily overcome; he was prevented from resorting to the last measures by the intelligence which reached him of the death of the king in Elymais (165).

The withdrawal of Lysias secured the fulfilment of the desires of the defenders of the faith in so far as it now enabled them to restore the Jerusalem worship to its previous condition. They lost no time in setting about the accomplishment of this. They were not successful indeed in wresting Acra from the possession of the Syrians, but they so occupied the garrison as to prevent it from interfering with the work of restoration. On 25th Kislev 165, the very day on which, three years before, "the abomination of desolation" had been inaugurated, the first sacrifice was offered on the new altar, and in commemoration of this the feast of the dedication was thenceforth celebrated.

As it was easy to see that danger still impended, the temple was put into a state of defence, as also was the town of Bethsur, where Lysias had been checked. But the favourable moment presented by the change of sovereign was made use of for still bolder attempts. Scattered over the whole of Southern Syria there were a number of Jewish localities on which the heathens now proceeded to wreak their vengeance. For the purpose of rescuing these oppressed co-religionists, and of bringing them in safety to Judæa, the Maccabees made a series of excursions, extending in some cases as far as to Lebanon and Damascus. Lysias had his hands otherwise fully occupied, and perhaps did not feel much disposed to continue the fight on behalf of the cultus of Zeus Olympios. Daily gaining in boldness, the Jews now took in hand also to lay regular siege to Acra. Then at last Lysias yielded to the pressure of Syrian and Jewish deputations, and determined to take serious steps (162). With a large force he entered Judæa, again from the south, and laid siege to Bethsur. Judas vainly attempted the relief of the fortress; he sustained near Bethzachariah a defeat in which his brother Eleazar perished. Bethsur was unable to hold out, being short of provisions on account of the sabbatic year. The Syrians advanced next to Jerusalem and besieged the temple; it also was insufficiently provisioned, and would soon have been compelled to surrender, had not Lysias been again called away at the critical moment by other exigencies. A certain Philip was endeavouring to oust him from the regency; as it was necessary for him to have his hands free in dealing with this new enemy, he closed a treaty with the temple garrison and the people at large, in accordance with which at once the political subjection and the religious freedom of the Jews were to be maintained. Thus the situation as it had existed before Antiochus IV. was restored. Only no attempt was made to replace Menelaus as high priest and ethnarch; this post was to be filled by Alcimus.

The concessions thus made by Lysias were inevitable; and even King Demetrius I., son of Seleucus IV., who towards the end of 162 ascended the throne and caused both Lysias and his ward to be put to death, had no thought of interfering with their religious freedom. But the Maccabees desired something more than the *status quo ante;* after having done their duty they were disinclined to retire in favour of Alcimus, whose sole claim lay in his descent from the old heathenishly-disposed high-priestly family. Alcimus was compelled to invoke the assistance of the king, who caused him to be installed by Bacchides. He was at once recognised by the scribes and Asidæans, for whom, with religious liberty, everything they wished had been secured; the claims to autonomy made by the Hasmonæans were of no consequence to them. Doubtless the masses also would ultimately have quietly accepted Alcimus, who of course refrained from interference with either law or worship, had he not abused the momentary power he derived from the presence of Bacchides to take a foolish revenge. The consequence of his action was that, as soon as Bacchides had turned his back, Alcimus was compelled to follow him. For the purpose of restoring him a Syrian army once more invaded Judæa under Nicanor (160), but first at Kapharsalama and afterwards at Bethhoron was defeated by Judas, and almost annihilated in the subsequent flight, Nicanor himself being among the slain (13th Adar = Nicanor's day). Judas was now at the acme of his prosperity ; about this time he concluded his (profitless) treaty with the Romans. But disaster was impending. In the month of Nisan, barely a month after the defeat of Nicanor, a new Syrian army under Bacchides entered Judæa from the north ; near Elasa, southward from Jerusalem, a decisive battle was fought which was lost by Judas, and in which he himself fell.

The religious war properly so called had already been brought once for all to an end by the convention of Lysias. If the struggle continued to be carried on, it was not for the faith but for the supremacy—less in the interests of the community than in those of the Hasmonæans. After the death of Judas the secular character which the conflict had assumed ever since 162 continually became more conspicuous. Jonathan Apphus fought for his house, and in doing so used thoroughly worldly means. The high-priesthood, *i.e.*, the ethnarchy, was the goal of his ambition. So long as Alcimus lived, it was far from his reach. Confined to the rocky fastnesses beside the Dead Sea, he had nothing for it but, surrounded by his faithful followers, to wait for better times. But on the death of Alcimus (159) the Syrians refrained from appointing a successor, to obviate the necessity of always having to protect him with military force. During the interregnum of seven years which followed, Jonathan again came more and more to the front, so that at last Bacchides concluded an armistice with him on the basis of the *status quo* (1 Macc. ix. 73). From his residence at Michmash Jonathan now exercised a *de facto* authority over the entire nation.

When accordingly Alexander Balas, a reputed son of Antiochus IV., rose against Demetrius, both rivals exerted themselves to secure the alliance of Jonathan, who did not fail to benefit by their competition. First of all, Demetrius formally recognised him as prince of Judah; in consequence of this he removed to Jerusalem, and expelled the heathen and heathenishly disposed, who continued to maintain a footing only in Acra and Bethsur. Next Alexander Balas conferred on him the title of "high priest of the nation and friend of the king;" in gratitude for which Jonathan went over to his side (152). He remained loyal, although Demetrius now made larger offers; he was justified by the event, for Demetrius I. had the worst of it and was slain (150). The victorious Balas heaped honours upon Jonathan, who maintained his fidelity, and fought successfully in his interests when in 147

Demetrius II., the son of Demetrius I., challenged a conflict. The high priest was unable indeed to prevent the downfall of Alexander in 145 ; but Demetrius II., won by presents, far from showing any hostility, confirmed him in his position in consideration of a tribute of 300 talents.

Jonathan was grateful to the king, as he showed by going with 3000 men to his aid against the insurgent Antiochenes. But when the latter drew back from his promise to withdraw the garrison from Acra, he went over to the side of Trypho, who had set up a son of Alexander Balas (Antiochus) as a rival. In the war which he now waged as Seleucid-strategus against Demetrius he succeeded in subduing almost the whole of Palestine. Meanwhile his brother Simon remained behind in Judæa, mastered the fortress of Bethsur, and resumed with great energy the siege of Acra. All this was done in the names of Antiochus and Trypho, but really of course in the interests of the Jews themselves. There were concluded also treaties with the Romans and Lacedæmonians, certainly not to the advantage of the Syrians.

Trypho sought now to get rid of the man whom he himself had made so powerful. He treacherously seized and imprisoned Jonathan in Ptolemais, and meditated an attack upon the leaderless country. But on the frontier Simon, the last remaining son of Mattathias, met him in force. All Trypho's efforts to break through proved futile; after skirting all Judæa from west to south, without being able to get clear of Simon, he at last withdrew to Peræa without having accomplished anything. On the person of Jonathan, whom he caused to be executed, he vented the spleen he felt on the discovery that the cause for which that prince had fought was able to gain the victory even when deprived of his help. Simon, in point of fact, was Jonathan's equal as a soldier and his superior as a ruler. He secured his frontier by means of fortresses, made himself master of Acra (141), and understood how to enable the people in time of peace to reap the advantages that result from successful war; agriculture, industry, and commerce (from the haven of Joppa) began to flourish vigorously. In grateful recognition of his services the high-priesthood and the ethnarchy were bestowed upon him as hereditary possessions by a solemn assembly of the people, " until a trustworthy prophet should arise."

Nominally the Seleucidæ still continued to possess the suzerainty. Simon naturally had detached himself from Trypho and turned to Demetrius II., who confirmed him in his position, remitted all arrears of tribute, and waived his rights for the future (142). The friendship of Demetrius II. and of his successor Antiochus Sidetes with Simon, however, lasted only as long as Trypho still remained in the way. But,

he once removed, Sidetes altered his policy. He
demanded of Simon the surrender of Joppa, Gazara,
and other towns, besides the citadel of Jerusalem,
as well as payment of all tribute resting due. The
refusal of these demands led to war, which in its
earlier stages was carried on with success, but the
scales were turned after the murder of Simon, when
Sidetes in person took the field against John Hyrcanus, Simon's son and successor. Jerusalem capitu-
lated. In the negotiations for peace the surrender
of all the external possessions of the Jews was insisted upon; the suzerainty of the Syrians became
once more a reality (135). But in 130 the powerful Antiochus Sidetes fell in an expedition against
the Parthians, and the complications anew arising
in reference to the succession to the Syrian throne
placed Hyrcanus in a position to recover what he
had lost, and to make new acquisitions. He subjugated Samaria and Idumæa, compelling the inhabitants of the latter to accept circumcision. Like his
predecessors, he too sought to secure the favour of
the Romans, but derived no greater benefit from the
effort than they had done. After a prosperous reign
of thirty years he died in 105. By Josephus he is
represented as a pattern of all that a pious prince
ought to be; by the rabbins as representing a
splendid high-priesthood. The darkness of the suc-
ceeding age lent a brighter colour to his image.

The external splendour of the Hasmonæan kingdom did not at once die away—the downfall of the Seleucidæ, which was its negative condition, being also a slow affair. Judah Aristobulus, the son of Hyrcanus, who reigned for only one year, was the first to assume the Greek title of royalty; Ituræa was in part subdued by him, and circumcision forced upon the inhabitants. His brother Jonathan (Jannæus) Alexander (104–79), in a series of continual wars, which were never very prosperous, nevertheless succeeded in adding the whole coast of Philistia (Gaza) as well as a great portion of Peræa to his hereditary dominions.[1] But the external enlargement of the structure was secured at the cost of its internal consistency.

From the time when Jonathan, the son of Mattathias, began to carry on the struggle no longer for the cause of God, but for his own interests, the scribes and the Asidæans, as we have seen, had withdrawn themselves from the party of the Maccabees. There can be no doubt that from their legal standpoint they were perfectly right in contenting themselves, as they did, with the attainment of religious liberty, and in accepting Alcimus. The Hasmonæans had no hereditary right to the highpriesthood, and their politics, which aimed at the establishment of a national monarchy, were contrary

[1] A number of half independent towns and communes lay as tempting subjects of dispute between the Seleucidæ, the Nabathæans or Arabs of Petra, and the Jews. The background was occupied by the Parthians and the Romans.

to the whole spirit and essence of the second theocracy. The presupposition of that theocracy was foreign domination; in no other way could its sacred, *i.e.*, clerical, character be maintained. God and the law could not but be forced into the background if a warlike kingdom, retaining indeed the forms of a hierocracy, but really violating its spirit at every point, should ever grow out of a mere pious community. Above all, how could the scribes hope to retain their importance if temple and synagogue were cast into the shade by politics and clash of arms? But under the first great Hasmonæans the zealots for the law were unable to force their way to the front; the enthusiasm of the people was too strong for them; they had nothing for it but to keep themselves out of the current and refuse to be swept along by it. Even under Hyrcanus, however, they gained more prominence, and under Jannæus their influence upon popular opinion was paramount. For under the last-named the secularisation of the hierocracy no longer presented any attractive aspects; it was wholly repellent. It was looked upon as a revolting anomaly that the king, who was usually in the field with his army, should once and again assume the sacred mantle in order to perform the sacrifice on some high festival, and that his officers, profane persons as they were, should at the same time be holders of the highest spiritual offices. The danger which in all this threatened "the idea of

158   ISRAEL AND JUDAH.   CHAP. XII.

Judaism" could not in these circumstances escape the observation of even the common people; for this idea was God and the law, not any earthly fatherland. The masses accordingly ranged themselves with ever-growing unanimity on the side of the Pharisees (*i.e.*, the party of the scribes) as against the Sadducees (*i.e.*, the Hasmonæan party).[1]

On one occasion, when Alexander Jannæus had returned to Jerusalem at the feast of tabernacles, and was standing in his priestly vestments before the altar to sacrifice, he was pelted by the assembled crowd of worshippers with citrons from the green branches they carried. By the cruelty with which he punished this insult he excited the populace to the highest pitch, and, when he lost his army in the disaster of Gadara, rebellion broke out. The Pharisees summoned the Syrian king Demetrius Eucærus; Jannæus was worsted and fled into the desert. But as he wandered in helplessness there, the patriotism of the people and sympathy for the heir of the Maccabees suddenly awoke; nature proved itself stronger than that consistency which

---

[1] פרוש means "separated," and refers perhaps to the attitude of isolation taken by the zealots for the law during the interval between 162 and 105. צדוקי (Σαδδουκαῖος) comes from צדוק (Σαδδούκ, LXX. in Ezekiel), the ancestor of the higher priesthood of Jerusalem (1 Kings ii. 35; 1 Sam. ii. 35; Ezek. xliv. 15), and designates the governing nobility. The original character of the opposition, as it appeared under Jannæus, changed entirely with the lapse of time, on account of the Sadducees' gradual loss of political power, till they fell at last to the condition of a sort of "fronde."

THE HASMONÆANS.

in the cause of the Divine honour had not shrunk from treason. The insurgents for the most part went over to the side of the fugitive king; the others he ultimately overpowered after a struggle which lasted through several years, Demetrius having withdrawn his intervention. The vengeance which he took on the Pharisees was a bloody one; their only escape was by voluntary exile. Thenceforward he had peace so far as they were concerned. His last years were occupied with the reacquisition of the conquests which he had been compelled to yield to the Arabs during the civil war. He died in the field at the siege of Ragaba in Peræa (79).

Under Queen Salome, his widow, matters were as if they had been specially arranged for the satisfaction of the Pharisees. The high-priesthood passed to Salome's son, Hyrcanus II.; she herself was only queen. In the management of external affairs her authority was absolute (*Ant.*, xiii. 16, 6); in home policy she permitted the scribes to wield a paramount influence. The common assertion, indeed, that the synedrium was at that time practically composed of scribes, is inconsistent with the known facts of the case; the synedrium at that time was a political and not a scholastic authority.[1] In its origin it was the municipal council of Jerusalem (so also the councils of provincial towns are called

---

[1] Kuenen, "Over de Samenstelling van het Sanhedrin," in *Proceedings of Royal Netherl. Acad.*, 1866.

synedria, Mark xiii. 9), but its authority extended over the entire Jewish community; alongside of the elders of the city the ruling priests were those who had the greatest number of seats and votes. John Hyrcanus appears to have been the first to introduce some scribes into its composition; it is possible that Salome may have increased their number, but even so this high court was far from being changed into a college of scribes like that at Jamnia. If the domination of the Pharisees at this time is spoken of, the expression cannot be understood as meaning that they already held all the public offices, but only at most that the holders of those offices found it necessary to administer and to judge in their spirit and according to their fundamental principles.

The party of the Sadducees (consisting of the old Hasmonæan officers and officials, who were of priestly family indeed, but attached only slight importance to their priestly functions) at length lost all patience. Led by Aristobulus, the second son of Jannæus, the leaders of the party came to the palace, and begged the queen to dismiss them from the court and to send them into the provinces. There they were successful in securing possession of several fortresses [1] in preparation for insurrection, a favourable opportunity for which they were

---

[1] Alexandrium, Coreæ, and similar citadels, which were at that time of great importance for Palestine and Syria.

THE HASMONÆANS.

watching. Such an opportunity occurred, it seemed to Aristobulus, as his mother lay on her death-bed. The commandants of the fortresses were at his orders, and by their assistance an army also, with which he accordingly advanced upon Jerusalem, and, on the death of Salome, made himself master of the situation (69). Hyrcanus was compelled to resign office. With this event the good understanding between the civil government and the Pharisees came to an end; the old antagonisms became active once more, and now began to operate for the advantage of a third party, the Idumæan Antipater, Hyrcanus's confidential friend. After the latter, aided by Antipater, had at length with great difficulty got himself into a position for asserting his rights against Aristobulus, the Pharisees could not do otherwise than rank themselves upon his side, and the masses joined them against the usurper. With the help of the Nabatæan monarch the effort to restore the elder brother to the supreme authority would doubtless have succeeded had not the Romans procured relief for Aristobulus, besieged as he was in Jerusalem (65), though without thereby recognising his claims. Pompey continued to delay a decision on the controversy in 64 also when the rival claimants presented themselves before him at Damascus; he wished first to have the Nabatæans disposed of, and to have free access to them through Judæa. This hesitation roused the suspicions of Aristobulus;

still he did not venture to take decisive action upon them. He closed the passes (to Mount Ephraim) against the Romans, but afterwards gave them up; he prepared Jerusalem for war, and then went in person to the Roman camp at Jericho, where he promised to open the gates of the city and also to pay a sum of money. But the Roman ambassadors found the gates barred, and had to return emptyhanded. Aristobulus thereupon was arrested, and siege was laid to Jerusalem. The party of Hyrcanus, as soon as it had gained the upper hand, surrendered the town; but the supporters of Aristobulus took their stand in the temple, and defended it obstinately. In June 63 the place was carried by storm; Pompey personally inspected the Holy of Holies, but otherwise spared the religious feelings of the Jews. But he caused the chief promoters of the war to be executed, and carried Aristobulus and his family into captivity. He abolished the kingship, but restored the high-priestly dignity to Hyrcanus. The territory was materially reduced in area, and made tributary to the Romans; the city was occupied by a Roman garrison.

CHAPTER XIII.

HEROD AND THE ROMANS.

HENCEFORWARD Roman intervention forms a constant disturbing factor in Jewish history. The struggle between the Pharisees and the Sadducees continued indeed to be carried on, but only because the momentum of their old feud was not yet exhausted. The Pharisees in a sense had been victorious. While the two brothers were pleading their rival claims before Pompey, ambassadors from the Pharisees had made their appearance in Damascus to demand the abolition of the kingship; this object had now to some extent been gained. Less ambiguous than the victory of the Pharisees was the fall of the Sadducees, who in losing the sovereignty of the Jewish state lost all real importance. But the intervention of the foreign element exercised its most powerful influence upon the temper of the lower classes. Though in times of peace the masses still continued to accept the guidance of the rabbins, their patriotism instantly burst into flame as soon as a pretender to the throne, belonging to the family of Aristobulus, appeared in Palestine. During the decennia which immediately followed, Jewish history was practically absorbed in vain attempts to restore the old Hasmonæan kingdom. Insurrections of steadily increasing dimensions were made in favour of Aristobulus, the representative of the national cause. For Hyrcanus was not regarded as a Hasmonæan at all, but merely as the creature of Antipater and the Romans. First, in the year 57, Alexander the son of Aristobulus broke into rebellion, then in 56 Aristobulus himself and his son Antigonus, and in 55 Alexander again. Antipater was never able to hold his own; Roman intervention was in every case necessary. The division of the Hasmonæan state into five "aristocracies" by Gabinius had no effect in diminishing the feeling of national unity cherished by the Jews of Palestine. Once again, after the battle of Carrhæ, a rising took place, which Cassius speedily repressed.

In 49 the great Roman civil war broke out; Cæsar instigated Aristobulus against Antipater, who in common with the whole East had espoused the cause of Pompey. But Aristobulus was poisoned by the opposite party while yet in Italy, and about the same time his son Alexander was also put to death at Antioch; thus the danger to Antipater passed away. After the battle of Pharsalus he went over to Cæsar's side, and soon after rendered him an important service by helping him out of his difficulties at Alexandria. By this means he earned the good-will of Cæsar towards the whole body of the Jews, and secured for himself (or Hyrcanus) a great extension of power and of territory. The five "synedria" or "aristocracies" of Gabinius were superseded, the most important conquest of the Hasmonæans restored, the walls of Jerusalem, which Pompey had razed, rebuilt.

However indisputable the advantages conferred by the rule of Antipater were, the Jews could not forget that the Idumæan, in name of Hyrcanus, the rightful heir of the Hasmonæans, was in truth setting up an authority of his own. The Sadducæan aristocracy in particular, which formerly in the synedrium had shared the supreme power with the high priest, endeavoured to restore reality once more to the nominal ascendancy which still continued to be attributed to the ethnarch and the synedrium. "When the authorities (οἱ ἐν τέλει) of the Jews saw how the power of Antipater and his sons was growing, their disposition towards him became hostile" (Jos., *Ant.*, xiv. 9, 3). They were specially jealous of the youthful Herod, to whom Galilee had been entrusted by his father. On account of the arbitrary execution of a robber chief Ezechias, who perhaps had originally been a Hasmonæan partisan, they summoned him before the synedrium, under the impression that it was not yet too late to remind him that he was after all but a servant. But the defiant demeanour of the culprit, and a threatening missive which at the same time arrived from Sextus Cæsar demanding his acquittal, rendered his judges speechless, nor did they regain their courage until they had heard the stinging reproaches of Sameas the scribe. Yet the aged Hyrcanus, who did not comprehend the danger that was threatening himself, postponed judgment upon Herod, and gave him opportunity to withdraw. Having been appointed strategus of Cœlesyria by Sextus Cæsar in the meanwhile he soon afterwards appeared before Jerusalem at the head of an army, and the authorities were compelled to address themselves in a conciliatory manner to his father, and to Phasael his brother, in order to secure his withdrawal.

The attempt to crush the serpent which had thus effected a lodgment in the Hasmonæan house came too late. The result of it simply was that the Herodians had now the advantage of being able to distinguish between Hyrcanus and his "evil counsellors." From that moment the downfall of the Sadducæan notables was certain. It was of no avail to them that after the battle of Philippi (42) they accused Herod and Phasael (Antipater having been murdered in 43) before Antony of having been helpful in every possible way to Cassius;

Antony declared himself in the most decisive manner for the two brothers. In their despair—for properly speaking they were not national fanatics, but only egoistic politicians—they ultimately made common cause with Antigonus the son of Aristobulus, and threw themselves into the arms of the Parthians, perceiving the interests of the Romans and of Herod to be inseparable (40). Fortune at first seemed to have declared in favour of the pretender. The masses unanimously took his side; Phasael committed suicide in prison; with a single blow Herod was stripped of all his following and made a helpless fugitive. He took refuge in Rome, however, where he was named king of Judæa by the senate, and after a somewhat protracted war he finally, with the help of the legions of Sosius, made himself master of Jerusalem (37). The captive Antigonus was beheaded at Antioch.

King Herod began his reign by reorganising the synedrium; he ordered the execution of forty-five of its noblest members, his most zealous opponents. These were the Sadducæan notables who long had headed the struggle against the Idumæan interlopers. Having thus made away with the leaders of the Jerusalem aristocracy, he directed his efforts to the business of corrupting the rest. He appointed to the most important posts obscure individuals, of priestly descent, from Babylon and Alexandria, and thus replaced with creatures of his own the old aristocracy. Nor did he rest content with this; in order to preclude the possibility of any independent authority ever arising alongside of his own, he abolished the life-tenure of the high-priestly office, and brought it completely under the control of the secular power. By this means he succeeded in relegating the Sadducees to utter insignificance. They were driven out of their native sphere—the political—into the region of theoretical and ecclesiastical discussion, where they continued, but on quite unequal terms, their old dispute with the Pharisees.

It was during the period of Herod's activity that the Pharisees, strictly speaking, enjoyed their greatest prosperity (Sameas and Abtalion, Hillel and Shammai); in the synedrium they became so numerous as almost to equal the priests and elders. Quite consistently with their principles they had abstained from taking any part in the life and death struggle for the existence of the national state. Their leaders had even counselled the fanatical defenders of Jerusalem to open the gates to the enemy; for this service they were treated with the highest honour by Herod. He made it part of his general policy to favour the Pharisees (as also the sect of the Essenes, insignificant though it was), it being his purpose to restrict the national life again within those purely ecclesiastical channels of activity which it had abandoned since the Maccabæan wars. However reckless his conduct in other respects, he was always scrupulously careful to avoid wounding religious susceptibilities (*Ant.*, xiv. 16, 3). But although the Pharisees might be quite pleased that the high-priesthood and the kingship were no longer united in one and the same person, and that interest in the law again overshadowed interest in politics, the populace for their part could never forgive Herod for overthrowing the old dynasty. That he himself, at least in religious profession, was a Jew, did not improve his position, but rather made it worse. It was not easy for him to stifle the national feeling after it had once been revived among the Jews; they could not forget the recent past, and objected to being thrust back into the time when foreign domination was endured by them as a matter of course. The Romans were regarded in quite a different light from that in which the Persians and the Greeks had been viewed, and Herod was only the client of the Romans.

His greatest danger seemed to arise from the still surviving members of the Hasmonæan family, to whom, as is easily understood, the national hopes clung. In the course of the earlier years of his reign he removed every one of them from his path, beginning with his youthful brother-in-law Aristobulus (35), after whom came his old patron Hyrcanus II. (30), then Mariamne his wife (29), and finally his stepmother Alexandra (28), the daughter of Hyrcanus and the widow of Alexander Aristobuli. Subsequently, in 25, he caused Costobarus and the sons of Babas to be executed. While thus occupied with domestic affairs, Herod had constant trouble also in his external relations, and each new phase in his political position immediately made itself felt at home. In the first instance he had much to suffer from Cleopatra, who would willingly have seen Palestine reduced under Egyptian domination once more, and who actually succeeded in inducing Antony to take from Herod several fair and valuable provinces of his realm. Next, his whole position was imperilled by the result of the battle of Actium; he had once more ranged himself upon the wrong side. But his tact did not fail him in winning Octavianus, as before it had made Antony his friend. In fact he reaped nothing but advantage from the great overturn which took place in Roman affairs; it rid him of Cleopatra, a dangerous enemy, and gave him in the new imperator a much better master than he had before.

During the following years he had leisure to carry out those splendid works of peace by which it was his aim to ingratiate himself with the emperor. He founded cities and harbours (Antipatris, Cæsarea), constructed roads, theatres, and temples, and subsidised far beyond his frontier all works of public utility. He taxed the Jews heavily, but in compensation promoted their material interests

HEROD AND THE ROMANS. 171

with energy and discretion, and built for them, from 20 or 19 B.C. onwards, the temple at Jerusalem. To gain their sympathies he well knew to be impossible. Apart from the Roman legions at his back his authority had its main support in his fortresses and in his system of espionage.

But just as the acme of his splendour had been reached, he himself became the instrument of a terrible vengeance for the crimes by which his previous years had been stained; as executioner of all the Hasmonæans, he was now constrained to be the executioner of his own children also. His suspicious temper had been aroused against his now grown-up sons by Mariamne, whose claims through their mother to the throne were superior to his own; his brother Pheroras and his sister Salome made it their special business to fan his jealousy into flame. To show the two somewhat arrogant youths that the succession was not so absolutely secure in their favour as they were supposing, the father summoned to his court Antipater, the exiled son of a former marriage. Antipater, under the mask of friendship, immediately began to carry on infamous intrigues against his half-brothers, in which Pheroras and Salome unconsciously played into his hands. For years he persevered alike in favouring and unfavouring circumstances with his part, until at last, by the machinations of a Lacedemonian, Eurycles, who had been bribed, Herod was induced to make condemn the sons of Mariamne at Berytus, and cause them to be strangled (Samaria, 7–6 B.C.). Not long afterwards a difference between Antipater and Salome led to the exposure of the former. Herod was compelled to drain the cup to the dregs; he was not spared the knowledge that he had murdered his children without a cause. His remorse threw him into a serious illness, in which his strong constitution wrestled long with death. While he lay at Jericho near his end he gave orders for the execution of Antipater also; and to embitter the joy of the Jews at his removal he caused their elders to be shut up together in the hippodrome at Jericho with the injunction to butcher them as soon as he breathed his last, that so there might be sorrow throughout the land. The latter order, however, was not carried out.

His death (4 B.C.) gave the signal for an insurrection of small beginnings which gradually spread until it ultimately infected all the people; it was repressed by Varus with great cruelty. Meanwhile Herod's connections were at Rome disputing about the inheritance. The deceased king (who was survived by several children of various marriages) had made a will, which was substantially confirmed by Augustus. By it his son Philip received the northern portion of the territory on the east of the Jordan along with the district of Paneas

HEROD AND THE ROMANS. 173

(Cæsarea Philippi); his thirty-seven years' reign over this region was happy. Another son, Herod Antipas, obtained Galilee and Peræa; he beautified his domains with architectural works (Sepphoris, Tiberias; Livias, Machærus), and succeeded by his fox-like policy in ingratiating himself with the emperors, particularly with Tiberius, for that very cause, however, becoming odious to the Roman provincial officials. The principal heir was Archelaus, to whom Idumæa, Judæa, and Samaritis were allotted; Augustus at first refused him the title of king. Archelaus had experienced the greatest difficulty in carrying through his claims before the emperor in face of the manifold oppositions of his enemies; the vengeance which he wreaked upon his subjects was so severe that in 6 A.D. a Jewish and Samaritan embassy besought the emperor for his deposition. Augustus assented, banishing Archelaus to Vienne, and putting in his place a Roman procurator. Thenceforward Judæa continued under procurators, with the exception of a brief interval (41–44 A.D.), during which Herod Agrippa I. united under his sway all the dominions of his grandfather.[1]

---

[1] Agrippa was the grandson of Mariamne through Aristobulus. Caligula, whose friendship he had secured in Rome, bestowed upon him in 37 the dominions of Philip with the title of king, and afterwards the tetrarchy of Antipas, whom he deposed and banished to Lugdunum (39). Claudius added the possessions of Archelaus. But the kingdom was again taken away from his son Agrippa II.

The termination of the vassal kingship resulted in manifest advantage to the Sadducees. The high priest and synedrium again acquired political importance; they were the responsible representatives of the nation in presence of the suzerain power, and conceived themselves to be in some sort lords of land and people (John xi. 48). For the Pharisees the new state of affairs appears to have been less satisfactory. That the Romans were much less oppressive to the Jews than the rulers of the house of Herod was a consideration of less importance to them than the fact that the heathen first unintentionally and then deliberately were guilty of the rudest outrages upon the law, outrages against which those sly half-Jews had well understood how to be on their guard. It was among the lower ranks of the people, however, that hatred to the Romans had its proper seat. On the basis of the views and tendencies which had long prevailed there, a new party was now formed, that of the Zealots, which did not, like the Pharisees, aim merely at the fulfilment of all righteousness, *i.e.*, of the law, and leave everything else in the hands of God, but was determined to take an active part in bringing about

(44), who, however, after the death of his uncle, Herod of Chalcis, obtained that principality for which at a later period (52) the tetrarchy of Philip was substituted. His sister Berenice is known as the mistress of Titus; another sister, Drusilla, was the wife of the procurator Felix. The descendants of Mariamne through Alexander held for some time an Armenian principality.

the realisation of the kingdom of God (Jos., *Ant.*, xviii. 1, 1).

As the transition to the new order of things was going on, the census of Quirinius took place (6–7 A.D.); it occasioned an immense excitement, which, however, was successfully allayed. On the withdrawal of Quirinius, Coponius remained behind as procurator of Judæa; he was followed, under Augustus, by Marcus Ambivius and Annius Rufus; under Tiberius, by Valerius Gratus (15–26 A.D.) and Pontius Pilatus (26–36 A.D.); under Caligula, by Marcellus (36–37) and Marullus (37–41 A.D.). The procurators were subordinate to the imperial legati of Syria; they resided in Cæsarea, and visited Jerusalem on special occasions only. They had command of the military, and their chief business was the maintenance of the peace and the care of the revenue. They interested themselves in affairs of religion only in so far as these had a political side; the temple citadel Antonia was constantly garrisoned with a cohort. The administration of justice appears to have been left to a very considerable extent in the hands of the synedrium, but it was not allowed to give effect to any capital sentence. At the head of the native authorities stood at this time not so much the actual high priest as the college of the chief priests. The actual office of high priest had lost its political importance in consequence of the frequency with which its holders were changed;

thus, for example, Annas had more influence than Caiaphas.

The principle of interfering as little as possible with the religious liberty of the Jews was rudely assailed by the Emperor Caius, who, like a second Antiochus, after various minor vexations, gave orders that his image should be set up in the temple of Jerusalem as in others elsewhere. It was entirely through the courage and tact of the Syrian governor P. Petronius that the execution of these orders was temporarily postponed until the emperor was induced by Agrippa I. to withdraw them. Caius soon afterwards died, and under the rule of Agrippa I., to whom the government of the entire kingdom of his grandfather was committed by Claudius, the Jews enjoyed much prosperity; in every respect the king was all they could wish. This very prosperity seems, however, to have caused them fresh danger. For it made them feel the government by procurators, which was resumed after the death of Agrippa I., to be particularly hard to bear, whatever the individual characters of these might be. They were Cuspius Fadus (from 44, under whom Theudas), Tiberius Alexander (the Romanised nephew of Philo, till 48), Cumanus (48–52, under whom the volcano already began to give dangerous signs of activity), and Felix (52–60). Felix, who has the honour to be pilloried in the pages of Tacitus, contrived to make the dispeace permanent. The influence of the

HEROD AND THE ROMANS.

two older parties, both of which were equally interested in the maintenance of the existing order, and in that interest were being drawn nearer to each other, diminished day by day. The masses broke loose completely from the authority of the scribes. The ruling nobility adapted itself better to the times; under the circumstances which then prevailed, it is not surprising that they became thoroughly secular and did not shrink from the employment of directly immoral means for the attainment of their ends. The Zealots became the dominant party. It was a combination of noble and base elements; superstitious enthusiasts (Acts xxi. 38), and political assassins, the so-called sicarii, were conjoined with honest but fanatical patriots. Felix favoured the sicarii in order that he might utilise them; against the others his hostility raged with indiscriminating cruelty, yet without being able to check them. The anarchy which he left behind him as a legacy was beyond the control of his able successor Porcius Festus (60–62), and the last two procurators, Albinus (62–64) and Gessius Florus, acted as if it had been their special business to encourage and promote it. All the bonds of social order were dissolved; no property was secure; the assassins alone prospered, and the procurators went shares with them in the profits.

It was inevitable that deep resentment against the Romans should be felt in every honest heart. At last it found expression. During his visit to Jerusalem in May 66, Florus laid hands upon the temple treasure; the Jews allowed themselves to go so far as to make a joke about it, which he avenged by giving over a portion of the city to be plundered, and crucifying a number of the inhabitants. He next insisted upon their kissing the rod, ordering that a body of troops which was approaching should be met and welcomed. At the persuasion of their leaders the Jews forced themselves even to this; but a constant succession of fresh insults and cruelties followed, till patience was quite exhausted at last, and in a violent street fight the Romans were so handled that the procurator withdrew from the town, leaving only the cohort in Antonia. Once again was an attempt at pacification made by Agrippa II., who hastened from Alexandria with this purpose, but the Jews could not bring themselves to make submission to Gessius Florus. It so happened that at this juncture the fortress of Masada on the Dead Sea fell into the hands of the Zealots; the courage of the party of action rose, and at the instance of the hot-headed Eleazar, the son of Ananias, a man still young, of highest priestly family, the sacrifice on behalf of the emperor was discontinued, *i.e.*, revolt was declared. But the native authorities continued opposed to a war. At their request King Agrippa sent soldiers to Jerusalem; at first they appeared to have some effect, but ultimately they were glad to make their escape in safety from the city. The cohort in Antonia was in like manner unable to hold its own; freedom was given it to withdraw; but, contrary to the terms of capitulation, it was put to the sword. The war party now signalised its triumph over all elements of opposition from within by the murder of the high priest Ananias.

A triumph was gained also over the outer foe. The Syrian legate, Cestius Gallus, appeared before Jerusalem in the autumn of 66, but after a short period raised the siege; his deliberate withdrawal was changed into a precipitate flight in an attack made by the Jews at Bethhoron. The revolt now spread irresistibly through all ranks and classes of the population, and the aristocracy found it expedient itself to assume the leadership. An autonomous government was organised, with the noblest members of the community at its head; of these the most important was the high priest Ananus.

Meanwhile Nero entrusted the conduct of the Jewish war to Vespasian, his best general. In the spring of 67 he began his task in Galilee, where the historian Josephus had command of the insurgents. The Jews entirely distrusted him and he them; in a short time the Romans were masters of Galilee, only a few strong places holding out against them. Josephus was besieged in Jotapata, and taken prisoner; the other places also were unable to hold out long. Such of the champions of freedom in Galilee as escaped betook themselves to Jerusalem; amongst these was the Zealot leader John of Giscala. There they told the story of their misfortunes, of which they laid the blame upon Josephus, and upon the aristocratic government, as having no heart for the common cause and having treachery for their motto. The Zealots now openly aimed at the overthrow of the existing government, but Ananus bravely withstood them, and pressed so hard on them that they summoned the Idumæans into the city to their aid. These honourable fanatics indeed withdrew again as soon as they had discovered that they were being used for sinister designs; but in the meanwhile they had accomplished the work of the Zealots. The old magistracy of Jerusalem was destroyed, Ananus with the heads of the aristocracy and very many other respectable citizens put to death. The radicals, for the most part not natives of the city, came into power; John of Giscala at their head tyrannised over the inhabitants.

While these events were taking place in Jerusalem, Vespasian had subdued the whole country, with the exception of one or two fortresses. But as he was setting about the siege of the capital, tidings arrived of the death of Nero, and the offensive was discontinued. For almost two years (June

68 to April 70), with a short break, war was suspended. When Vespasian at the end of this period became emperor, he entrusted to Titus the task of reducing Jerusalem. There in the interval the internal struggle had been going on, even after the radicals had gained the mastery. As a counterpoise to John of Giscala the citizens had received the guerilla captain Simon bar Giora into the city; the two were now at feud with each other, but were alike in their rapacity towards the citizens. John occupied the temple, Simon the upper city lying over against it on the west. For a short time a third entered into competition with the two rivals, a certain Eleazar who had separated from John and established himself in the inner temple. But just as Titus was beginning the siege (Easter 70) John contrived to get rid of this interloper.

Titus attacked from the north. After the lower city had fallen into his hands, he raised banks with a view to the storm of the temple and the upper city. But the defenders, who were now united in a common cause, taught him by their vigorous resistance that his object was not to be so quickly gained. He therefore determined to reduce them by famine, and for this end completely surrounded the city with a strong wall. In the beginning of July he renewed the attack, which he directed in the first instance against the temple. The tower of Antonia fell on the 5th, but the temple continued to be held notwithstanding; until the 17th the daily sacrifice continued to be offered. The Romans succeeded in gaining the outer court in August only. To drive them out, the Jews in the night of August 10–11 made a sortie, but were compelled to retire, the enemy forcing their way behind them into the inner court. A legionary flung a firebrand into an annexe of the temple, and soon the whole structure was in flames.[1] A terrible slaughter of the defenders ensued, but John with a determined band succeeded in cutting his way out, and by means of the bridge over the Tyropœon valley made his escape into the upper city.

No attack had as yet been directed against this quarter; but famine was working terrible ravages among the crowded population. Those in command, however, refused to capitulate unless freedom to withdraw along with their wives and children were granted. These terms being withheld, a storm, after the usual preparations on the part of the Romans, took place. The resistance was feeble; the strong towers were hardly defended at all; Simon bar Giora and John of Giscala now thought only of their personal safety. In the unprotected city the

---

[1] So Josephus (*W. J.*, vi. 4, 5). According to Sulpicius Severus, on the other hand, the destruction of the temple was no accident, but commanded by Titus. Sulpicius probably derived his information from Tacitus. Compare Bernays, "Ueber die Chronik des Sulpicius Severus," 1861, pp. 48–61 (*Gesammelte Abhandlungen*, ii. 159–181), and Mommsen, *Römische Geschichte*, v. p. 539, *n.* 1.

Roman soldiers spread fire and slaughter unchecked (September 7, 70).

Of those who survived also some were put to death; the rest were sold or carried off to the mines and amphitheatres. The city was levelled with the ground; the tenth legion was left behind in charge. Titus took with him to Rome for his triumphal procession Simon bar Giora and John of Giscala, along with seven hundred other prisoners, also the sacred booty taken from the temple, the candlestick, the golden table, and a copy of the Torah. He was slightly premature with his triumph; for some time elapsed, and more than one bloody battle was necessary, before the rebellion was completely stifled. It did not come wholly to an end until the fall of Masada (April 73).

CHAPTER XIV.

THE RABBINS.

EVEN now Palestine continued for a while to be the centre of Jewish life, but only in order to prepare the way for its transition into thoroughly cosmopolitan forms. The development of thought sustained no break on account of the sad events which had taken place, but was only directed once more in a consistent manner towards these objects which had been set before it from the time of the Babylonian exile. On the ruins of the city and of the temple the Pharisaic Judaism which rests upon the law and the school celebrated its triumph. National fanaticism indeed was not yet extinguished, but it burnt itself completely out in the vigorous insurrection led by Simeon bar Koziba (Bar Cochebas, 132–135). That a conspicuous rabbin, Akiba, should have taken part in it, and have recognised in Simeon the Messiah, was an inconsistency on his part which redounds to his honour.

Inasmuch as the power of the rabbins did not depend upon the political or hierarchical forms of the old commonwealth, it survived the fall of the latter.

THE RABBINS.

Out of what hitherto had been a purely moral influence something of an official position now grew. They formed themselves into a college which regarded itself as a continuation of the old synedrium, and which carried forward its name. At first its seat was at Jamnia, but it soon removed to Galilee, and remained longest at Tiberias. The presidency was hereditary in the family of Hillel, with the last descendants of whom the court itself came to an end.[1] The respect in which the synedrial president was held rapidly increased; like Christian patriarchs under Mahometan rule, he was also recognised by the imperial government as the municipal head of the Jews of Palestine, and bore the secular title of the old high priests (nasi, ethnarch, patriarch). Under him the Palestinian Jews continued to form a kind of state within a state until the 5th century. From the non-Palestinian Jews he received offerings of money.[2]

The task of the rabbins was so to reorganise Judaism under the new circumstances that it could continue to assert its distinctive character. What of external consistency had been lost through the extinction of the ancient commonwealth required to

---

[1] The following is the genealogy of the first Nasi:—Gamaliel ben Simeon (Jos., *Vit.*, 38) ben Gamaliel (Acts v. 34, xxii. 3) ben Simeon ben Hillel. The name Gamaliel was that which occurred most frequently among the patriarchs; see *Cod. Theod*, xvi. 8, 22.

[2] Comp. Gothofredus on *Cod. Theod.*, xvi. 8, and Morinus, *Exerc. bibl.*, ii. 3, 4.

be compensated for by an inner centralisation proportionately stronger. The separation from everything heathenish become more pronounced than before; the use of the Greek language was of necessity still permitted, but at least the Septuagint was set aside by Aquila, inasmuch as it had now become the Christian Bible.[1] For to this period also belongs the definitive separation between the synagogue and the church; henceforward Christianity could no longer figure as a Jewish sect. Intensified exclusiveness was accompanied by increased internal stringency. What at an earlier period had still remained to some extent fluid now became rigidly fixed; for example, an authentic text of the canon was now established, and at the same time the distinction between canon and apocrypha sharply drawn. The old tendency of the scribes to leave as little as possible free to the individual conscience, but to bring everything within the scope of positive ordinance, now celebrated its greatest triumphs. It was only an apparent movement in the direction of liberty, if regulations which had become quite impossible were now modified or cancelled. The most influential of the rabbins were indeed the least solicitous about the maintenance of what was old, and had no hesitation in introducing numerous and thoroughgoing innovations; but the conservatives R. Eliezer ben Hyrcanus and R. Ishmael

[1] *Cod. Justin.*, Nov. 146.

ben Elisha were in truth more liberal-minded than the leaders of the party of progress, notably than R. Akiba. Even the Ultramontanes have never hesitated at departures from the usage of the ancient and mediæval Church; and the Pharisaic rabbins were guided in their innovations by liberal principles no more than they. The object of the new determinations was simply to widen the domain of the law in a consistent manner, to bring the individual entirely under the iron rule of system. But the Jewish communities gave willing obedience to the hierarchy of the rabbins; Judaism had to be maintained, cost what it might. That the means employed were well adapted to the purpose of maintaining the Jews as a firmly compacted religious community, even after all bonds of nationality had fallen away, cannot be doubted. But whether the attainment of this purpose by incredible exertion was a real blessing to themselves and the world may very well be disputed.

One consequence of the process of intellectual isolation, and of the effort to shape everything in accordance with hard and fast rules and doctrines, was the systematisation and codification of juristic and ritual tradition, a work with which a beginning was made in the century following the destruction of Jerusalem. Towards the end of the 2nd century the Pharisaic doctrine of Hillel, as it had been further matured by Akiba, was codified and elevated to the position of statute law by the patriarch Rabban Judah the Holy (Mishna). But this was only the first stage in the process of systematising and fixing tradition. The Mishna became itself the object of rabbinical comment and supplement; the Tannaim, whose work was registered in the Mathnetha (Mishna, $\delta\epsilon\upsilon\tau\epsilon\rho\omega\sigma\iota\varsigma$ = doctrine), were followed by the Amoraim, whose work in turn took permanent shape in the Gemara (= doctrine). The Palestinian Gemara was reduced to writing in perhaps the 4th or 5th century; unfortunately it has been preserved to us only in part, but appears to have reached the Middle Ages in a perfect state. Even thus the process which issued in the production of the Talmud was not yet completed; the Babylonian Amorian carried it forward for some time longer, until at last at the rise of Islam the Babylonian Gemara was also written down.

In the 5th century Palestine ceased to be the centre of Judaism. Several circumstances conspired to bring this about. The position of the Jews in the Roman Empire had changed for the worse with the elevation of Christianity to be the religion of the state; the large autonomy which until then they had enjoyed in Palestine was now restricted; above all, the family of the patriarchs, which had come to form a veritable dynasty, became extinct.[1] But this did not make an end of what may be called the

[1] Comp. Gothofredus on *Cod. Theod.*, xvi. 8, 29, *ad voc.* "post excessum patriarcharum."

THE RABBINS.

Jewish church-state; henceforward it had its home in Babylonia. From the period of the exile, a numerous and coherent body of Jews had continued to subsist there; the Parthians and Sassanidæ granted them self-government; at their head was a native prince (Resh Galutha—can be clearly traced from 2nd century A.D. onwards) who, when the Palestinian patriarchate came to an end, was left without a rival. This remarkable relic of a Jewish commonwealth continued to exist until the time of the Abassides.[1] Even as early as the beginning of the 3rd century A.D. certain rabbins, at their head Abba Areka (Rab), had migrated from Palestine and founded a settlement for learning in the law in Babylonia. The schools there (at Pumbeditha, Sora, Nahardea) prospered greatly, vied with those of Palestine, and continued to exist after the cessation of the latter, when the patriarchate became extinct; thus they had the last word in the settlement of doctrine.

Alongside of the settlement of tradition went another task, that of fixing the letters of the consonantal text of the Bible (by the Massora), its vowel pronunciation (by the punctuation), and its translation into the Aramaic vernacular (Targum). Here also the Babylonians came after the Palestinians, yet of this sort of erudition Palestine continued to be the headquarters even after the 5th century.

[1] See Nöldeke, *Tabari*, 68, 118, and Kremer, *Culturgeschichte des Orients unter den Chalifen*, i. 188, ii. 176.

With this task—that of attaining to the greatest possible conformity to the letter and of continuing therein—the inner development of Jewish thought came to an end. The later Hebrew literature, which does not fall to be considered here, contributed very few new elements; in so far as an intellectual life existed at all among the Jews of the Middle Ages, it was not a growth of native soil, but proceeded from the Mahometan or Latin culture of individuals. The Kabbala at most, and even it hardly with justice, can be regarded as having been a genuine product of Judaism. It originated in Palestine, and subsequently flourished chiefly in the later Middle Ages in Spain, and, like all other methodised nonsense, had strong attractions for Christian scholars.

CHAPTER XV.

THE JEWISH DISPERSION.

SOMETHING still remains to be said with reference to the diaspora. We have seen how it began; in spite of Josephus (*Ant.*, xi. 5, 2), it is to be carried back not to the Assyrian but merely to the Babylonian captivity; it was not composed of Israelites, but solely of citizens of the southern kingdom. It received its greatest impulse from Alexander, and then afterwards from Cæsar. In the Græco-Roman period Jerusalem, at the time of the great festival, presented the appearance of a veritable Babel (Acts ii. 9-11); with the Jews themselves were mingled the proselytes (Acts ii. 11), for even already that religion was gaining considerable conquests among the heathen. As King Agrippa I. writes to the Emperor Caius, "Jerusalem is the metropolis not only of Judæa but of very many lands, on account of the colonies which on various occasions (ἐπὶ καιρῶν) it has sent out into the adjoining countries of Egypt, Phœnicia, Syria, and Cœlesyria, and into the more remote Pamphylia, Cilicia, the greater part of Asia Minor as far as to Bithynia and the remotest parts of Pontus; likewise into Europe—Thessaly, Bœotia, Macedonia, Ætolia, Attica, Argos, Corinth, most parts (and these the fairest) of the Peloponnesus. Nor are the Jewish settlements confined to the mainland only; they are found also in the more important islands, Eubœa, Cyprus, Crete. I do not insist on the countries beyond the Euphrates, for with few exceptions all of them, Babylon and the fertile regions around it, have Jewish inhabitants."[1] In the west of Europe also they were not wanting; many thousands of them lived in Rome. In those cities where they were at all numerous they, during the imperial period, formed separate communities. Josephus has preserved a great variety of documents in which the Roman authorities recognise their rights and liberties (especially as regards the Sabbath rest and the observance of festivals). Of greatest importance was the community in Alexandria; according to Philo, a million of Jews had their residence there under an ethnarch, for whom a gerusia was afterwards substituted by Augustus. The extent to which this diaspora was helpful in the diffusion of Christianity, the manner in which the mission of the apostles everywhere attached itself to the synagogues

[1] Philo, *Legatio ad Gaium*, § 36.

and proseuchai, is well known from the New Testament. That the Christians of the 1st century had much to suffer along with the Jews is also a familiar fact. For at this period, in other respects more favourable to them than any other had previously been, the Jews had occasionally to endure persecution. The emperors, taking umbrage at their intrusiveness, more than once banished them from Rome (Acts xviii. 2). The good will of the native population they never secured; they were most hated in Egypt and Syria, where they were strongest.[1]

---

[1] The place taken by the Jewish element in the world of that time is brilliantly set forth by Mommsen in his *History of Rome* (bk. v. ch. ii.; Eng. tr. iv. p. 538 *seq.*, 1866)—"How numerous even in Rome the Jewish population was already before Cæsar's time, and how closely at the same time the Jews even then kept together as fellow-countrymen, is shown by the remark of an author of this period, that it was dangerous for a governor to offend the Jews in his province, because he might then certainly reckon on being hissed, after his return, by the populace of the capital. Even at this time the predominant business of the Jews was trade. . . . At this period too we encounter the peculiar antipathy of the Occidentals towards this so thoroughly Oriental race and their foreign opinions and customs. This Judaism, although not the most pleasing feature in the nowhere pleasing picture of the mixture of nations which then prevailed, was, nevertheless, an historical element developing itself in the natural course of things, . . . which Cæsar, just like his predecessor Alexander, fostered as far as possible. . . . They did not, of course, contemplate placing the Jewish nationality on an equal footing with the Hellenic or Italo-Hellenic. But the Jew, who has not, like the Occidental, received the Pandora's gift of political organisation, and stands substantially in a relation of indifference to the state,

The position of the Jews in the Roman Empire was naturally not improved by the great risings under Nero, Trajan (in Cyrene, Cyprus, Mesopotamia), and Hadrian. The East, strictly so called, became more and more their proper home. The Christianisation of the empire helped still further in a very special way to detach them from the Western world.[1] They sided with the Persians against the Byzantines; in the year 614 they were even put in possession of Jerusalem by Chosroes, but were not long able to hold their own against Heraclius.[2] With Islam also they found themselves in greater sympathy than with Christianity, although they were cruelly treated by Mahomet in Arabia, and driven by Omar out of the Hejaz, and notwithstanding the facts that they were as matter of course excluded from citizenship, and that they were held by Moslems as a whole in greater contempt than the Christians. They throve especially

---

who, moreover, is as reluctant to give up the essence of his national idiosyncrasy as he is ready to clothe it with any nationality at pleasure and to adapt himself up to a certain degree to foreign habits—the Jew was, for this very reason as it were, made for a state which was to be built on the ruins of a hundred living polities, and to be endowed with a somewhat abstract and, from the outset, weakened nationality. In the ancient world also Judaism was an effective leaven of cosmopolitanism and of national decomposition."

[1] For a brief time only were they again favoured by Julian the Apostate; comp. Gibbon, chap. xxiii.

[2] Gibbon, chap. xlvi.

well on what may be called the bridge between East and West, in Mauretania and Spain, where they were the intellectual intermediaries between the Arab and the Latin culture. In the Sephardim and Ashkenazim the distinction between the subtler Oriental and the more conservative Western Jews has maintained itself in Europe also. From the 8th century onwards Judaism put forth a remarkable side shoot in the Khazars on the Volga; if legend is to be believed, but little was required at one time to have induced the Russians to accept the Jewish rather than the Christian faith.

In the West the equal civil rights which Caracalla had conferred on all free inhabitants of the empire came to an end, so far as the Jews were concerned, in the time of Constantine. The state then became the secular arm of the Church, and took action, though with less severity, against Jews just as against heretics and pagans. As early as the year 315, Constantine made conversion from Christianity to Judaism a penal offence, and prohibited Jews, on pain of death, from circumcising their Christian slaves. These laws were re-enacted and made more severe by Constantius, who attached the penalty of death to marriages between Jews and Christians. Theodosius I. and Honorius, indeed, by strictly prohibiting the destruction of synagogues, and by maintaining the old regulation that a Jew was not to be summoned before a court of justice on a Sabbath-day, put a check upon the militant zeal of the Church, by which even Chrysostom, for example, allowed himself to be carried away at Antioch. But Honorius rendered them ineligible for civil or military service, leaving open to them only the bar and the decurionate, the latter being a *privilegium odiosum*. Their liberty to try cases by their own law was curtailed; the cases between Jews and Christians were to be tried by Christian judges only. Theodosius II. prohibited them from building new synagogues, and anew enforced their disability for all state employments. Most hostile of all was the orthodox Justinian, who, however, was still more severe against Pagans and Samaritans.[1] He harassed the Jews with a law enjoining them to observe Easter on the same day as the Christians, a law which it was of course found impossible to carry out.[2]

In the Germanic states which arose upon the ruins of the Roman empire, the Jews did not fare badly on the whole. It was only in cases where the state was dominated by the Catholic Church, as, for

---

[1] *Cod. Theod.*, xvi. 8: "De Judæis, Cœlicolis, et Samaritanis;" *Cod. Just.*, i. 9: "De Judæis et Cœlicolis." With regard to these cœlicolæ, see Gothofredus on *Cod. Theod.*, xvi. 8, 9, and also J. Bernays, "Ueber die Gottesfürchtigen bei Juvenal," in the *Comm. Philol. in hon. Th. Mommsen*, 1877, p. 163.

[2] Gibbon, chap. xlvii.

example, among the Spanish Visigoths, that they were cruelly oppressed; among the Arian Ostrogoths, on the other hand, they had nothing to complain of. One thing in their favour was the Germanic principle that the law to be applied depended not on the land but on the nationality, as now in the East Europeans are judged by the consuls according to the law of their respective nations. The autonomy of the Jewish communities, which had been curtailed by the later emperors, was now enlarged once more under the laxer political and legal conditions. The Jews fared remarkably well under the Frankish monarchy; the Carolingians helped them in every possible way, making no account of the complaints of the bishops. They were allowed to hold property in land, but showed no eagerness for it; leaving agriculture to the Germans, they devoted themselves to trade. The market was completely in their hands; as a specially lucrative branch of commerce they still carried on the traffic in slaves, which had engaged them even in ancient times.[1]

---

[1] Agobardus Lugdunensis (9th century) wrote four pamphlets against the Jews. He was no superstitious fanatic, but one of the weightiest and most enlightened ecclesiastics of the Middle Ages. Compare, further, Stobbe, *Die Juden in Deutschland* (Brunsw. 1866), p. 199 *seq.*, *notes* 6 and 8, and Georg Jakob, *Ueber die Handelsartikel, welche die Araber aus den nordischen Ländern bezogen*

Meanwhile the Church was not remiss in seeking constantly repeated re-enactments of the old imperial laws, in the framing of which she had had paramount influence, and which she now incorporated with her own canon law.[1] Gradually she succeeded in attaining her object. In the later Middle Ages the position of the Jews in the Christian society deteriorated. Intercourse with them was shunned; their isolation from being voluntary became compulsory; from the 13th century onwards they were obliged to wear, as a distinctive mark (more necessary in the East than in the West), a round or square yellow badge on their breast.[2] The difference of religion elicited a well-marked religious hate with oft-repeated deadly outbreaks, especially during the period of the crusades, and afterwards when the Black Death was raging (1348-50). Practical consequences like these the Church of course did not countenance;

(Berlin, 1891), p. 8 *seq*. The Jews carried on a trade in Slavonian children in the Mahometan East by way of Spain; they castrated the boys.

[1] Compare Decret. i., dist. 45, c. 3; Decret. ii., caus. 23, quæst. 8, c. 9, caus. 28, qu. 1, c. 10-12; Decret. iii., de consecr., dist. 4, c. 93; Decret. Greg. 5, 6 ("De Judæis, Sarracenis, et eorum servis"), 5, 19, 18; Extrav. commun. 5, 2.

[2] Comp. Du Cange, s. v. "Judæi;" also Reuter, *Gesch. d. Aufklärung im Mittelalter*, i. 154 *seq*. In spite of all the legal restrictions laid upon them, the Jews still continued to have great influence with the princes, and more especially with the popes, of the Middle Ages.

the popes set themselves against persecutions of the Jews,[1] but with imperfect success. The popular aversion rested by no means exclusively on religious considerations; worldly motives were also present. The Jews of that period had in a still higher degree than now the control of financial affairs in their hands; and they used it without scruple. The Church herself had unintentionally given them a monopoly of the money market, by forbidding Christians to take interest.[2] In this way the Jews became rich indeed, but at the same time made themselves still more repugnant to the Christian population than they previously were by reason of their religion.

Having, according to the later mediæval system,

---

[1] Decret. ii. 23, 8, 9. Alexander II. omnibus episcopis Hispaniæ: Dispar . . . est Judæorum et Sarracenorum causa; in illos enim, qui Christianos persequuntur et ex urbibus et propriis sedibus pellunt, juste pugnatur, hi vero ubique servire parati sunt.

[2] Decret. Greg. v. 19, 18. Innocent III. in name of the Lateran Council: Quanto amplius Christiana religio ab exactione compescitur usurarum, tanto gravius super his Judæorum perfidia insolescit, ita quod brevi tempore Christianorum exhauriunt facultates. Volentes igitur in hac parte prospicere Christianis, ne a Judæis immaniter aggraventur, synodali decreto statuimus, ut, si de cætero quocunque prætextu Judæi a Christianis graves immoderatasve usuras extorserint, Christianorum eis participium subtrahatur, donec de immoderato gravamine satisfecerint competenter. . . . Principibus autem injungimus, ut propter hoc non sint Christianis infesti, sed potius a tanto gravamine studeant cohibere Judæos.

no rights in the Christian state, the Jews were tolerated only in those territories where the sovereign in the exercise of free favour accorded them protection. This protection was granted them in many quarters, but never for nothing; numerous and various taxes, which could be raised or changed in a perfectly arbitrary way, were exacted in exchange. But in countries where the feeling of nationality attained to a vigorous development, the spirit of toleration was speedily exhausted; the Jews were expelled by the act of the state. England was the first kingdom in which this occurred (1290); France following in 1395, Spain and Portugal in 1492 and 1495. In this way it came about that the Holy Roman Empire—Germany, Italy, and adjoining districts—became the chief abode of the Jews.[1] In the anarchy which here prevailed they could best maintain their separate attitude, and if they were expelled from one locality they readily found refuge in some other. The emperor had indeed the right of extirpating them altogether (with the exception of a small number to be left as a memorial); but, in the first place, he had in various ways given up this right to the states of the empire, and, moreover, his pecuniary resources

---

[1] The Polish Jews are German Jews who migrated in the Middle Ages to Poland, but have maintained to the present day their German speech, a mediæval South-Frankish dialect, of course greatly corrupted.

THE JEWISH DISPERSION. 201

were so small that he could not afford to want the tax which the Jews as his "servi cameræ" paid him for protecting their persons and property. In spite of many savage persecutions the Jews maintained their ground, especially in those parts of Germany where the political confusion was greatest. They even succeeded in maintaining a kind of autonomy by means of an arrangement in virtue of which civil processes which they had against each other were decided by their own rabbins in accordance with the law of the Talmud.

The Jews, through their having on the one hand separated themselves, and on the other hand been excluded on religious grounds from the Gentiles, gained an internal solidarity and solidity which has hitherto enabled them to survive all the attacks of time. The hostility of the Middle Ages involved them in no danger; the greatest peril has been brought upon them by modern times, along with permission and increasing inducements to abandon their separate position. It is worth while to recall on this point the opinion of Spinoza,[1] who was well able to form a competent judgment:—"That the Jews have maintained themselves so long in spite of their dispersed and disorganised condition is not at all to be wondered at, when it is considered how

[1] *Tract. Theol. Polit.* c. 4, *ad fin.*

they separated themselves from all other nationalities in such a way as to bring upon themselves the hatred of all, and that not only by external rites contrary to those of other nations, but also by the sign of circumcision, which they maintain most religiously. Experience shows that their conservation is due in a great degree to the very hatred which they have incurred. When the king of Spain compelled the Jews either to accept the national religion or to go into banishment, very many of them accepted the Roman Catholic faith, and in virtue of this received all the privileges of Spanish subjects, and were declared eligible for every honour; the consequence was that a process of absorption began immediately, and in a short time neither trace nor memory of them survived. Quite different was the history of those whom the king of Portugal compelled to accept the creed of his nation; although converted, they continued to live apart from the rest of their fellow-subjects, having been declared unfit for any dignity. So great importance do I attach to the sign of circumcision also in this connection, that I am persuaded that it is sufficient by itself to maintain the separate existence of the nation for ever." The persistency of the race may, of course, prove a harder thing to overcome than Spinoza has supposed; but nevertheless he will be found to have spoken truly in declaring that the so-called emancipation of the Jews must inevitably lead to the extinction of Judaism wherever the process is extended beyond the political to the social sphere. For the accomplishment of this centuries may be required.

APPENDIX.

APPENDIX.[1]

Judaism and Christianity.

The post-Deuteronomic legislation is not addressed to the people, but to the congregation; its chief concern is the regulation of worship. Political matters are not touched upon, as they are in the hands of a foreign lord. The hierocracy is taken for granted as the constitution of the congregation. The head of the cultus is the head of the whole; the high priest takes the place of the king. The other priests, though his brothers or his sons, are officially subordinate to him, as bishops to the supreme pontiff. They, again, are distinguished from the Levites, not only by their office, but also by their noble blood, though the Levites belong by descent to the clergy, of which they form the lowest grade. The material basis of the hierarchical pyramid is furnished by the contributions of the laity, which are required on a scale which cannot be called modest. Such is the outward aspect of the rule of the holy in Israel. Inwardly, the ideal of holiness governs the whole of life by means of a net of ceremonies and observances which separate the Jew from the natural man. "Holy" means almost the same as

---

[1] See Wellhausen, *Skizzen* i. (1884), p. 86 *seq.*

"exclusive." Originally the term was equivalent to divine, but now it is used chiefly in the sense of religious, priestly, as if the divine were to be known from the worldly, the natural, by outward marks.

It had so fallen out, even before the exile, that the reform of the theocracy which the prophets demanded began in the cultus; and after the exile this tendency could not fail to be persisted in. The restoration of Judaism took place in the form of a restoration of the cultus. Yet this restoration was not a relapse into the heathen ways which the prophets had attacked. The old meaning of the festivals and of the sacrifices had long faded away, and after the interruption of the exile they would scarcely have blossomed again of themselves; they had become simply statutes, unexplained commands of an absolute will. The cultus had no longer any real value for the Deity; it was valuable only as an exercise of obedience to the law. If it had been at first the bond connecting Israel with heathenism, now, on the contrary, it was the shield behind which Judaism retreated to be safe from heathenism. There was no other means to make Judaism secure; and the cultus was nothing more than a means to that end. It was the shell around the faith and practice of the fathers, around the religion of moral monotheism, which it alone preserved until it could become the common property of the world. The great public worship gave the new theocracy a firm centre, thus keeping it one and undivided, and helped it to an organisation. But of more importance was the minor private cultus of pious exercises, which served to Judaise the whole life of every individual. For the centre of gravity of Judaism was in the individual. Judaism was gathered from scattered elements, and it depended on the labour of the individual to make himself a Jew. This is the secret of the persistence of Judaism, even in the diaspora. The initiatory act of circumcision, which conferred an indelible character, was not the only safeguard; the whole of the education which followed that act went to guard against the disintegrating effects of individualism. This is the real significance of the incessant discipline, which consisted mainly in the observance of laws of purity, and generally of regulations devised to guard against sin. For what holiness required was not to do good, but to avoid sin. By the sin and trespass offerings, and by the great day of atonement, this private cultus was connected with that of the temple; hence it was that all these institutions fitted so admirably into the system. The whole of life was directed in a definite sacred path; every moment there was a divine command to fulfil, and this kept a man from following too much the thoughts and desires of his own heart. The Jews trained themselves with an earnestness and zeal which have no parallel to create, in the absence of all natural conditions, a holy nation which should answer to the law, the concrete embodiment of the ideals of the prophets.

In the individualism thus moulded into uniformity lay the chief difference which separated the new period from the old. The aim was universal culture by the law, that the prophecy should be fulfilled which says: "They shall all be taught of God." This universal culture was certainly of a peculiar kind, and imposed more troublesome observances than the culture of our day. Yet the strange duties which the law imposed were not universally felt to be a heavy burden. Precepts which were plain and had to do with something outward were very capable of being kept; the harder they seemed at first, the easier were they when the habit had been formed. A man saw that he was doing what was prescribed, and did not ask what was the use of it. The ever-growing body of regulations even came to be felt as a sort of emancipation from self. Never had the individual felt himself so responsible for all he did and left undone, but the responsibility was oppressive, and it was well that there should be a definite precept for every hour of his life, thus diminishing the risk of his going astray. Nor must we forget that the Torah contained other precepts than those which were merely ceremonial. The kernel did not quite harden into wood inside the shell; we must even acknowledge that moral sentiment gained very perceptibly in this period both in delicacy and in power. This also is connected with the fact that religion was not, as before, the custom of the people, but the work of the individual. A further consequence of this was, that men began to reflect upon religion. The age in question saw the rise of the so-called "Wisdom," of which we possess examples in the Book of Job, in the Proverbs of Solomon and of the Son of Sirach, and in Ecclesiastes. This wisdom flourished not only in Judah, but also at the same time in Edom; it had the universalistic tendency which is natural to reflection. The Proverbs of Solomon would scarcely claim attention had they arisen on Greek or Arabian soil; they are remarkable in their pale generality only because they are of Jewish origin. In the Book of Job, a problem of faith is treated by Syrians and Arabians just as if they were Jews. In Ecclesiastes religion abandons the theocratic ground altogether, and becomes a kind of philosophy in which there is room even for doubt and unbelief. But speculation did not on the whole take away from depth of feeling; on the contrary, individualism helped to make religion more intense. This is seen strikingly in the Psalms, which are altogether the fruit of this period. Even the sacrificial practice of the priests was made subjective, being incorporated in the Torah, *i.e.*, made a matter for every one to learn. Though the laity could not take part in the ceremony, they were at least to be thoroughly informed in all the minutiæ of the system; the law was a means of interesting every one in the great public sacrificial procedure. Another circumstance also tended to remove the centre of gravity of the temple service from the priests to the congregation. The service of song, though executed by choirs of singers, was yet in idea the song of the congregation, and came to be of more importance than the acts of worship which it accompanied and inspired. The Holy One of Israel sat enthroned, not on the smoke-pillars of the altar, but in the praises of the congregation pouring out its heart in prayer; the sacrifices were merely the external occasion for visiting the temple, the real reason for doing so lay in the need for the strength and refreshment to be found in religious fellowship.

By the Torah religion came to be a thing to be learned. Hence the need of teachers in the church of the second temple. As the scribes had codified the Torah, it was also their task to imprint it on the minds of the people, and to fill their life with it; in this way they at the same time founded a supplementary and changing tradition, which kept pace with the needs of the time. The place of teaching was the synagogue; there the law and the prophets were read and explained on the Sabbath. The synagogue and the Sabbath were of more importance than the temple and the festivals; and the moral influence of the scribes transcended that of the priests, who had to be content with outward power and dignity. The rule of religion was essentially the rule of the law, and consequently the Rabbis at last served themselves heirs to the hierarchs. At the same time, while the government of the law was acknowledged in principle, it could at no time be said to be even approximately realised in fact. The high-born priests who stood at the head of the theocracy, cared chiefly, as was quite natural, for the maintenance of their own supremacy. And there were sheep in the flock not to be kept from breaking out, both in the upper and in the lower classes of society; the school could not suppress nature altogether. It was no trifle even to know the six hundred and thirteen commandments of the written law, and the incalculable number of the unwritten. Religion had to be made a profession of, if it was to be practised aright. It became an art, and thereby at the same time a matter of party : the leaders of the religious were of course the scribes. The division became very apparent in the time of the Hellenisation which preceded the Maccabæan revolt; at that period the name of Pharisees, *i.e.*, the

Separated, came into vogue for the party of the religious. But the separation and antipathy between the godly and the ungodly had existed before this, and had marked the life of the congregation after the exile from the very first.

It was the law that gave the Jewish religion its peculiar character. But, on the other hand, a hope was not wanting to that religion; the Jews cherished the prospect of a reward for the fulfilling of the law. This hope attached itself to the old prophecies, certainly in a very fantastic way. The Jews had no historical life, and therefore painted the old time according to their ideas, and framed the time to come according to their wishes. They stood in no living relation with either the past or the future; the present was not with them a bridge from the one to the other; they did not think of bestirring themselves with a view to the kingdom of God. They had no national and historical existence, and made no preparations to procure such a thing for themselves; they only hoped for it as a reward of faithful keeping of the law. Yet they dreamed not only of a restoration of the old kingdom, but of the erection of a universal world-monarchy, which should raise its head at Jerusalem over the ruins of the heathen empires. They regarded the history of the world as a great suit between themselves and the heathen. In this suit they were in the right; and they waited for right to be done them. If the decision was delayed, their sins were the reason; Satan was accusing them before the throne of God, and causing the judgment to be postponed. They were subjected to hard trials, and if tribulation revived their hopes, with much greater certainty did it bring their sins into sorrowful remembrance. Outward circumstances still influenced in the strongest way their religious mood.

But the old belief in retribution which sought to justify itself in connection with the fortunes of the congregation proved here also unequal to the strain laid upon it. Even in Deuteronomy it is maintained that the race is not to suffer for the act of an individual. Jeremiah's contemporaries thought it monstrous that because the fathers had eaten sour grapes the teeth of the children should be set on edge. Ezekiel championed, in a notable way, the cause of individualism on this ground. He denounced the Jews who had remained in Palestine, and who regarded themselves as the successors of the people of Jehovah because they dwelt in the Holy Land and had maintained some sort of existence as a people. In his view only those souls which were saved from the dispersion of the exile were to count as heirs of the promise; the theocracy was not to be perpetuated by the nation, but by the individual righteous men. He maintained that each man lived because of his own righteousness, and died because of his own wickedness; nay more, the fate of the individual corresponded even in its fluctuations to his moral worth at successive times. The aim he pursued in this was a good one; in view of a despair which thought there was nothing for it but to pine and rot away because of former sins, he was anxious to maintain the freedom of the will, *i.e.*, the possibility of repentance and forgiveness. But the way he chose for this end was not a good one; on his showing it was chance which ultimately decided who was good and who was wicked. The old view of retribution which allowed time for judgment to operate far beyond the limit of the individual life had truth in it, but this view had none. Yet it possessed one merit, that it brought up a problem which had to be faced, and which was a subject of reflection for a long time afterwards.

The problem assumed the form of a controversy as to the principle on which piety was rewarded—this controversy taking the place of the great contest between Israel and the heathen. Were the wicked right in saying that there was no God, *i.e.*, that He did not rule and judge on earth? Did He in truth dwell behind the clouds, and did He not care about the doings of men? In that case piety would be an illusion. Piety cannot maintain itself if God makes no difference between the godly and the wicked, and has nothing more to say to the one than to the other; for piety is not content to stretch out its hands to the empty air, it must meet an arm descending from heaven. It must have a reward, not for the sake of the reward, but in order to be sure of its own reality, in order to know that there is a communion of God with men and a road which leads to it. The usual form of this reward is the forgiveness of sins; that is the true motive of the fear of God. That is to say, as long as it is well with him, the godly man does not doubt, and so does not require any unmistakable evidence by which he may be justified and assured of the favour of God. But misfortune and pain destroy this certainty. They are accusers of sin, God's warnings and corrections. Now is the time to hold fast the faith that God leads the godly to repentance, and destroys the wicked, that He forgives the sin of the former, but punishes and avenges that of the latter. But this faith involves a hope of living to see better things; the justification of which the good man is sure must at last be attested by an objective judgment of God before the whole world, and the godly delivered from his sufferings. Hence the constant anxiety and restlessness of his conscience ; the judgment passed upon him is ultimately to be gathered from the external world, and he can never be sure how it is to turn out. And a principle is also at stake the whole time, namely, the question whether godliness or ungodliness is right in its fundamental conviction. Each individual case at once affects the generality, the sufferings of one godly person touch all the godly. When he recovers and is saved, they triumph; when he succumbs, or seems to succumb, to death, they are cast down, unless in this case they should change their minds about him and hold him to be a hypocrite whom God has judged and unmasked. In the same way they are all hurt at the prosperity of an ungodly man, and rejoice together at his fall, not from jealousy or pleasure in misfortune for its own sake, but because in the one case their faith is overturned, while in the other it is confirmed.

The tortures incident to this curious oscillation between believing and seeing are set forth in the most trenchant way in the Book of Job. Job, placed in an agonising situation, condemned without hope to the death of sinners, and yet conscious of his godliness, demands vengeance for his blood unjustly shed. But the vengeance is to be executed on God, and in such a case who can be the avenger ? There is no one but God Himself, and thus the striking thought arises, that God will be the champion against God of his innocence, after having first murdered it. From the God of the present he appeals to the God of the future; but the identity between these two is yet maintained, and even now, the God who slays him is the sole witness of his innocence, in which the world and his friends have ceased to believe. God must be this now if He is to avenge him in the future. An inner antinomy is in this way impersonated; the view of the friends is one of which the sufferer himself cannot divest himself; hence the conflict in his soul. But, supported by the unconquerable power of his good conscience, he struggles till he frees himself from the delusion; he believes more firmly in the direct testimony of his conscience than in the evidence of facts and the world's judgment about him, and against the dreadful God of reality, the righteous God of faith victoriously asserts Himself.

Job in the end reaches the conclusion that he cannot understand God's ways. This is a negative expression of the position that he holds fast, in spite of all, to himself and to God; that is to say, that not outward experience, but inner feeling, is to decide. This inner feeling of the union of God with the godly meets us also in some of the Psalms, where, in spite of depression arising from untoward circumstances, it maintains itself as a reality which cannot be shaken, which temptations and doubts even tend to strengthen. It was a momentous step when the soul in its relations to God ventured to take its stand upon itself, to trust itself. This was an indirect product of prophecy, but one of not less importance than its direct product, the law. The prophets declared the revelation of God, which had authority for all, but along with this they had their own personal experience, and the subjective truth of which they thus became aware proved a more powerful solvent and emancipator than the objective one which formed the subject of their revelation. They preached the law to deaf ears, and laboured in vain to convert the people. But if their labour had produced no outward result, it had an inner result for them. Rejected by the people, they clung the more closely to Jehovah, in the conviction that the defeated cause was favoured by Him, that He was with them and not with the people. Especially with Jeremiah did prophecy, which is designed primarily to act on others, transform itself into an inner converse with the Deity, which lifted him above all the annoyances of his life. In this relation, however, there was nothing distinctively prophetical, just because it was a matter of the inner life alone, and was sufficient for itself; it was just the essence of the life of religion that the prophets thus brought to view and helped to declare itself. The experience of Jeremiah propagated itself and became the experience of religious Israel. This was the power by which Israel was enabled to rise again after every fall; the good conscience towards God, the profound sentiment of union with Him, proved able to defy all the blows of outward fortune. In this strength the servant, despised and slain, triumphed over the world; the broken and contrite heart was clothed and set on high with the life and power of the Almighty God. This divine spirit of assurance rises to its boldest expression in the 73rd Psalm: "Nevertheless I am continually with Thee; Thou holdest me by my right hand ; Thou guidest me with Thy counsel, and drawest me after Thee by the hand. If I have Thee, I desire not heaven nor earth ; if my flesh and my heart fail, Thou, God, art for ever the strength of my heart, and my portion."

The life surrendered is here found again in a higher life, without any expression of hope of a hereafter. In the Book of Job we do indeed find a trace of this hope, in the form that even after the death of the martyr, God may still find opportunity to justify him and pronounce him innocent ; yet this idea is only touched on as a distant possibility, and is at once dropped. Certainly the position of that man is a grand one who can cast into the scale against death and devil his inner certainty of union with God—so grand indeed that we must in honesty be ashamed to repeat those words of the 73rd Psalm. But the point of view is too high. The danger was imminent of falling from it down into the dust and seeking comfort and support in the first earthly experience that might offer, or, on the other hand, sinking into despair. Subjective feeling was not enough of itself to outbid the contradictions of nature ; the feeling must take an objective form—a world other than this one, answering the demands of morality, must build itself up to form a contrast to the world actually existing. The merit of laying the foundations for this religious metaphysic which the time called for belongs, if not to the Pharisees themselves, at least to the circles from which they immediately proceeded. The main features of that metaphysic first appear in the Book of Daniel, where we find a doctrine of the last things. We have already spoken of the transition from the old prophecy to apocalypse. With the destruction of the nation and the cessation of historical life, hope was released from all obligation to conform to historical conditions; it no longer set up an aim to which even the present might aspire, but ran riot after an ideal, at the advent of which the historical development would be suddenly broken off. To be pious was all the Jews could do at the time; but it caused them bitter regret that they had no part in the government of the world, and in thought they anticipated the fulfilment of their wishes. These they raised to an ever higher pitch in proportion as their antagonism to the heathen became more pronounced, and as the world became more hostile to them and they to the world. As the heathen empires stood in the way of the universal dominion of Israel, the whole of them together were regarded as one power, and this world-empire was then set over against the kingdom of God, *i.e.*, of Israel. The kingdom of God was entirely future; the fulfilling of the law did not prepare the way for it, but was only a statutory condition for its coming, not related to it inwardly as cause to effect. History was suddenly to come to a stop and cease. The Jews counted the days to the judgment; the judgment was the act by which God would at once realise all their wishes. The view thus taken of the world's history was a very comprehensive one and well worked out from its principle, yet of an entirely negative character; the further the world's history went wilfully away from its goal, the nearer did it unintentionally approach its goal.

In this view, however, the earth always continued to

be the place of hope; the kingdom of God was brought by the judgment into earthly history; it was on earth that the ideal was to be realised. A step further, and the struggle of the dualism of the earth was preluded in the skies by the angels, as the representatives of the different powers and nations. In this struggle a place was assigned to Satan; at first he was merely the accuser whom God Himself had appointed, and in this character he drew attention to the sins of the Jews before God's judgment-seat, and thereby delayed the judicial sentence in their favour; but ultimately (though this took place late, and is not met with in the Book of Daniel) he came to be the independent leader of the power opposed to God, God's cause being identified with that of the Jews. But as this prelude of the struggle took place in heaven, its result was also anticipated. The kingdom of God is on earth a thing of the future, but even now it is preserved in heaven with all its treasures, one day to descend from there to the earth. Heaven is the place where the good things of the future are kept, which are not and yet must be; that is its original and true signification.

But the most important question came at last to be, how individuals were to have part in the glory of the future? How was it with the martyrs who had died in the expectation of the kingdom of God, before it came? The doctrine of the *zakuth* was formed: if their merit was not of service to themselves, it was yet of service to others. But this was a solution with which individualism could not rest content. And what of the ungodly? Were they to escape from wrath because they died before the day of judgment? It was necessary that the departed also should be allowed to take some part in the coming retribution. Thus there arose—it is remarkable how late and how slowly—the doctrine of the resurrection of the dead, that the kingdom of God might not be of service only to those who happened to be alive at the judgment. Yet at first this doctrine was only used to explain particularly striking cases. The Book of Daniel says nothing of a general resurrection, but speaks in fact only of a resurrection of the martyrs and a punishment of the wicked after death. With all this the resurrection is not the entrance to a life above the earth but to a second earthly life, to a world in which it is no longer the heathen but the Jews who bear rule and take the lead. Of a general judgment at the last day, or of heaven and hell in the Christian sense, the Jews know nothing, though these ideas might so easily have suggested themselves to them.

It is not easy to find points of view from which to pronounce on the character of Judaism. It is a system, but a practical system, which can scarcely be set forth in relation to one leading thought, as it is an irregular product of history. It lives on the stores of the past, but is not simply the total of what had been previously acquired; it is full of new impulses, and has an entirely different physiognomy from that of Hebrew antiquity, so much so that it is hard even to catch a likeness. Judaism is everywhere historically comprehensible, and yet it is a mass of antinomies. We are struck with the free flight of thought and the deep inwardness of feeling which are found in some passages in the Wisdom and in the Psalms; but, on the other hand, we meet with a pedantic asceticism which is far from lovely, and with pious wishes the greediness of which is ill-concealed; and these unedifying features are the dominant ones of the system. Monotheism is worked out to its furthest consequences, and at the same time is enlisted in the service of the narrowest selfishness; Israel participates in the sovereignty of the One God. The Creator of heaven and earth becomes the manager of a petty scheme of salvation; the living God descends from His throne to make way for the law. The law thrusts itself in everywhere; it commands and blocks up the access to heaven; it regulates and sets limits to the understanding of the divine working on earth. As far as it can, it takes the soul out of religion and spoils morality. It demands a service of God, which, though revealed, may yet with truth be called a self-chosen and unnatural one, the sense and use of which are apparent neither to the understanding nor the heart. The labour is done for the sake of the exercise; it does no one any good, and rejoices neither God nor man. It has no inner aim after which it spontaneously strives and which it hopes to attain by itself, but only an outward one, namely, the reward attached to it, which might as well be attached to other and possibly even more curious conditions. The ideal is a negative one, to keep one's self from sin, not a positive one, to do good upon the earth; the morality is one which scarcely requires for its exercise the existence of fellow-creatures. Now pious exercises can dam up life and hold it in bounds, they may conquer from it more and more ground, and at last turn it into one great Sabbath, but they cannot penetrate it at the root. The occupation of the hands and the desire of the heart fall asunder. There is no connection between the practice and the ideal.

The Gospel develops hidden impulses of the Old Testament, but it is a protest against the ruling tendency of Judaism. Jesus understands monotheism in a different way from His contemporaries. They think in connection with it of the folly of the heathen and their great happiness in calling the true God their own; He thinks of the claims, not to be disputed or avoided, which the Creator makes on the creature. He feels the reality of God dominating the whole of life, He breathes in the fear of the Judge who requires an account for every idle word, and has power to destroy body and soul in hell. "No man can serve two masters; ye cannot serve God and Mammon; where your treasure is, there will your heart be also." This monotheism is not to be satisfied with stipulated services, how many and great soever; it demands the whole man, it renders doubleness of heart and hypocrisy impossible. Jesus casts ridicule on the works of the law, the washing of hands and vessels, the tithing of mint and cummin, the abstinence even from doing good on the Sabbath. Against unfruitful self-sanctification He sets up another principle of morality, that of the service of one's neighbour. He rejects that lofty kind of goodness, which says to father and mother, If I dedicate what I might give to you, that will be best even for you yourselves; He contends for the weightier matters in the law, for the common morality which sees its aim in the furtherance of the well-being of others, and which commends itself at once to the heart of every one.

Just this natural morality of self-surrender does He call the law of God; that supernatural morality which thinks to outbid this, He calls the commandment of men. Thus religion ceases to be an art which the Rabbis and Pharisees understand better than the unlearned people which know nothing of the law. The arrogance of the school fares ill at the hands of Jesus; He will know nothing of the partisanship of piety or of the separateness of the godly; He condemns the practice of judging a man's value before God. Holiness shrinks from contact with sinners, but He helps the world of misery and sin; and there is no commandment on which He insists more than that of forgiving others their debts as one hopes for forgiveness himself from Heaven. He is most distinctly opposed to Judaism in His view of the kingdom of heaven, not as merely the future reward of the worker, but as the present goal of effort, it being the supreme duty of man to help it to realise itself on earth, from the individual outwards. Love is the means, and the community of love the end.

Self-denial is the chief demand of the Gospel; it means the same thing as that repentance which must precede entrance into the kingdom of God. The will thereby breaks away from the chain of its own acts, and makes an absolutely new beginning not conditioned by the past. The causal nexus which admits of being traced comes here to an end, and the mutual action, which cannot be analysed, between God and the soul begins. This miracle does not require to be understood, only to be believed, in order to take place. With men it is impossible, but with God it is possible. Jesus not only affirmed this, but proved it in His own person. The impression of His personality convinced the disciples of the fact of the forgiveness of their sins and of their second birth, and gave them courage to believe in a new divine life and to live it. He had in fact lost His life and saved it; He could do as He would. He had found freedom and personality in God, who alone is master of Himself, and lifts those up to Himself who seek after Him.

Jesus works in the world and for the world, but with His faith He stands above the world and outside it. He can sacrifice Himself for the world because He asks nothing from the world, but has attained in retirement with God to equanimity and peace of soul. And further, the entirely supra-mundane position, at which Jesus finds courage and love to take an interest in the world, does not lead Him to anything strained or unnatural. He trusts God's Providence, and resigns Himself to His will, He takes up the attitude of a child towards Him, and loves best to call Him the Heavenly Father. The expression is simple, but the thing signified is new. He first knows Himself, not in emotion but in sober quietness, to be God's child; before Him no one ever felt himself to be so, or called himself so. He is the first-born of the Father, yet, according to His own view, a first-born among many brethren. For He stands in this relation to God not because His nature is unique, but because He is man; He uses always and emphatically this general name of the race to designate His own person. In finding the way to God for Himself He has opened it to all; along with the nature of God He has at the same time discovered in Himself the nature of man.

Eternity extends into the present with Him, even on

earth He lives in the midst of the kingdom of God; even the judgment He sees inwardly accomplished here below in the soul of man. Yet He is far from holding the opinion that he who loves God aright does not desire that God should love him in return. He teaches men to bear the cross, but He does not teach that the cross is sweet and that sickness is sound. A coming reconciliation between believing and seeing, between morality and nature, everywhere forms the background of His view of the world; even if He could have done without it for His own person, yet it is a thing He takes for granted, as it is an objective demand of righteousness. So much is certain; for the rest the eschatology of the New Testament is so thoroughly saturated with the Jewish ideas of the disciples, that it is difficult to know what of it is genuine.

Jesus was so positive that He did not feel any need for breaking old idols, so free that no restraint could depress Him, so unconquerable that even under the load of the greatest accumulations of rubbish He could still breathe. This ought ye to do, He said, and not to leave the other undone; He did not seek to take away one iota, but only to fulfil. He never thought of leaving the Jewish community. The Church is not His work, but an inheritance from Judaism to Christianity. Under the Persian domination the Jews built up an unpolitical community on the basis of religion. The Christians found themselves in a position with regard to the Roman Empire precisely similar to that which the Jews had occupied with regard to the Persian; and so they also founded, after the Jewish pattern, in the midst of the state which was foreign and hostile to them, and in which they could not feel themselves at home, a religious community as their true fatherland. The state is always the presupposition of the Church; but it was at first, in the case both of the Jewish and of the Christian Church, a foreign state. The original meaning of the Church thus disappeared when it no longer stood over against the heathen world-power, it having become possible for the Christians also to possess a natural fatherland in the nation. In this way it became much more difficult to define accurately the spheres of the state and the Church respectively, regarding the Church as an organisation, not as an invisible community of the faithful. The distinction of religious and secular is a variable one; every formation of a religious community is a step towards the secularisation of religion; the religion of the heart alone remains an inward thing. The tasks of the two competing organisations are not radically different in their nature; on the one side it may be said that had not the Christian religion found civil order already in existence, had it come, like Islam, in contact with the anarchy of Arabia instead of the Empire of Rome it must have founded not the Church, but the state; on the other side it is well known that the state has everywhere entered into possession of fields first reclaimed to cultivation by the Church. Now we must acknowledge that the nation is more certainly created by God than the Church, and that God works more powerfully in the history of the nations than in Church history. The Church, at first a substitute for the nation which was wanting, is affected by the same evils incident to an artificial cultivation as meet us in Judaism. We cannot create for ourselves our sphere of life and action; better that it should be a natural one, given by God. And yet it would be unjust to deny the permanent advantages of the differentiation of the two. The Church will always be able to work in advance for the state of the future. The present state unfortunately is in many respects only nothing more than a barrier to chaos; if the Church has still a task, it is that of preparing an inner unity of practical conviction, and awakening a sentiment, first in small circles, that we belong to each other.

Whether she is to succeed in this task is certainly the question. The religious individualism of the Gospel is, and must remain for all time, the true salt of the earth. The certainty that neither death nor life can separate us from the love of God drives out that fear which is opposed to love; an entirely supra-mundane faith lends courage for resultless self-sacrifice and resigned obedience on earth. We must succeed: *sursum corda!*